quick and easy
party cakes

hamlyn

quick and easy
party cakes

Joanna Farrow and Sara Lewis

First published in Great Britain in 2006 by Hamlyn,
a division of Octopus Publishing Group Ltd
2–4 Heron Quays
London E14 4JP

Copyright © Octopus Publishing Group 2006

ISBN-13: 978-0-600-61420-3
ISBN-10: 0-600-61420-4

A CIP catalogue record for this book is available from the British Library.

Printed and bound in China.

10 9 8 7 6 5 4 3 2 1

contents

introduction

Nothing completes a party quite like a wonderful homemade cake. It adds a personal touch to any celebration, and, whether it's a birthday, anniversary, graduation or wedding, a lovingly prepared cake that's been personalized for the occasion will be enjoyed and appreciated by all.

Many people avoid making their own cakes and resort to bought varieties instead because they lack the confidence and skills required to make a cake from scratch. With the help of this book, you'll soon realize that baking, icing and decorating your own party cakes is surprisingly easy, as well as being an extremely rewarding experience. If you're short of time, a shop-bought base can be quickly transformed into a fabulous party cake with one of the many ideas in the following chapters.

Once you've mastered the basics you'll be creating more adventurous cakes in no time at all, and you'll soon be taking a cake along with you to every party. We'll take you through some basic

cake recipes, as well as providing information on icing and decorating, there are also some top tips to ensure you get great results every time. The recipes cover every imaginable type of party and celebration, and they've all been selected because they don't require any specialist skills. So, even if you've never baked a cake before, you can try your hand at easy but impressive cakes for a children's party, such as the Chocolate Hedgehogs (page 74), or more sophisticated cakes for special occasions, such as a Winter Wedding Cake (page 144). Baking your own party cakes is a rewarding experience and you can be absolutely sure that your friends and family will thank you for it, too!

essential equipment

The recipes in this book are all easy to make, and you shouldn't really require a lot of specialist equipment. You'll probably find that you already have a lot of things in your kitchen, but, if you do need to buy anything extra, it's probably best to visit a specialist cake-decorating shop. This is the best place to go for specialist equipment, such as cutters in all shapes and sizes, as well as for ready-made cake decorations, icing and food colourings. Many companies also offer a mail order service if you don't have a local shop, and, of course, you'll find plenty of ordering services on the Internet.

Here we have listed some of the basic equipment and utensils that you'll need for many of the recipes – this should be plenty to get you going.

- **Large and small palette knives (essential for spreading icing)**
- **Kitchen scales**
- **Rolling pin**
- **Pastry brush**
- **Scissors**
- **Selection of bowls in various sizes**
- **Sieve**
- **Cake tins (at least one round and one square, with loose bases)**
- **Muffin tins (for fairy cakes and cup cakes)**
- **Baking tins**
- **Greaseproof and nonstick baking paper**
- **Baking sheets**
- **Whisk**

basic cake recipes

With many of the recipes in this book you have the option either to use a shop-bought cake as the base or to make your own. Because it's so easy to make the actual cake yourself, it's always better to do so. Although, if you're short of time, shop-bought cakes are perfectly acceptable, though they tend to be quite small and shallow. If you make your own cake, you have complete control over the size and type of cake that you use, and the end result will be far superior, as well as cheaper. Why not make a big batch of cakes at one time and then freeze them until you're ready to complete them with icing and decorations? On the following pages there are a selection of basic cake recipes that are easy to make, and you will also find some quick variations.

basic sponge cake

square cake	12 cm (5 inch)	15 cm (6 inch)	18 cm (7 inch)	20 cm (8 inch)	23 cm (9 inch)
round cake	15 cm (6 inch)	18 cm (7 inch)	20 cm (8 inch)	23 cm (9 inch)	25 cm (10 inch)
serves	8	12	16	20	24
cooking time	40 minutes	50–60 minutes	1 hour	1–1¼ hours	1¼–1½ hours

ingredients

unsalted butter, softened	175 g (6 oz)	225 g (7½ oz)	300 g (10 oz)	375 g (12 oz)	475 g (15 oz)
caster sugar	175 g (6 oz)	225 g (7½ oz)	300 g (10 oz)	375 g (12 oz)	475 g (15 oz)
medium eggs	3	4	5	6	8
milk	2 tablespoons	3 tablespoons	4 tablespoons	5 tablespoons	150 ml (¼ pint)
self-raising flour	250 g (8 oz)	300 g (10 oz)	400 g (13 oz)	625 g (1¼ lb)	750 g (1½ lb)

flavour variations

vanilla

vanilla extract	1 teaspoon	2 teaspoons	1 tablespoon	4 teaspoons	2 tablespoons

orange or lemon
substitute juice for milk

orange or lemon rind	rind of 1	rind of 1	rind of 1½	rind of 2	rind of 3
orange or lemon juice	2 tablespoons	3 tablespoons	4 tablespoons	5 tablespoons	150 ml (¼ pint)

chocolate
substitute cocoa powder for equal amount of flour

cocoa powder	25 g (1 oz)	40 g (1½ oz)	50 g (2 oz)	65 g (2½ oz)	75 g (3 oz)

1 Use a wooden spoon or electric whisk to cream the butter and sugar together until light and fluffy. Lightly beat the eggs with the milk in a separate bowl. Gradually beat the eggs and milk into the creamed mixture, alternating with the flour.

2 Turn the mixture into the prepared tin (see page 19) and level the surface. Bake in a preheated oven, 160°C (325°F), Gas Mark 3, for the time indicated in the chart or until a skewer, inserted in the centre, comes out clean. Leave the cake in the tin for 10 minutes, then transfer it to a wire rack to cool.

rich chocolate cake

square cake	12 cm (5 inch)	18 cm (7 inch)	23 cm (9 inch)
round cake	15 cm (6 inch)	20 cm (8 inch)	25 cm (10 inch)
serves	10	18	24
cooking time	1 hour	1¼ hours	1½ hours
ingredients			
cocoa powder	75 g (3 oz)	125 g (4oz)	175 g (6 oz)
boiling water	250 ml (8 fl oz)	375 ml (13 fl oz)	575 ml (18 fl oz)
unsalted butter, softened	125 g (4 oz)	200 g (7 oz)	325 g (11 oz)
light muscovado sugar	275 g (9 oz)	400 g (13 oz)	700 g (1½ lb)
eggs, beaten	2	3	5
plain flour	200 g (7 oz)	300 g (10 oz)	500 g (1 lb)
baking powder	1 teaspoon	1½ teaspoons	2½ teaspoons

1 Put the cocoa powder in a bowl and gradually whisk in the boiling water until smooth. Leave to cool.

2 Beat together the butter and sugar until they are creamy. Gradually beat in the eggs, a little at a time, adding a little of the flour to prevent curdling. Sift the remaining flour over the bowl with the baking powder. Use a large metal spoon to fold in the flour. Stir in the cocoa mixture.

3 Turn the mixture into the prepared tin (see page 19). Bake in a preheated oven, 180°C (350°F), Gas Mark 4, for the time stated in the chart or until the crust is just firm. For a good, moist texture the centre of the cake should have a slight wobble when it comes out of the oven.

4 Leave to cool in the tin, then wrap and store for up to 3 days in a cool place or freeze.

rich fruit cake

square cake	12 cm (5 inch)	18 cm (7 inch)	23 cm (9 inch)
round cake	15 cm (6 inch)	20 cm (8 inch)	25 cm (10 inch)
serves	14	24	40
cooking time	2–2½ hours	3½–3¾ hours	4–4½ hours
ingredients			
unsalted butter, softened	150 g (5 oz)	250 g (8 oz)	425 g (14 oz)
light muscovado sugar	150 g (5 oz)	250 g (8 oz)	425 g (14 oz)
eggs, beaten	3	5	8
plain flour	200 g (7 oz)	325 g (11 oz)	625 g (1¼ lb)
ground mixed spice	2 teaspoons	1 tablespoon	2 tablespoons
stem ginger, chopped	25 g (1 oz)	40 g (1½ oz)	65 g (2½ oz)
luxury mixed dried fruit	625 g (1¼ lb)	1 kg (2 lb)	2 kg (4 lb)
blanched chopped almonds	50 g (2 oz)	75 g (3 oz)	100 g (3½ oz)

1 Beat together the butter and sugar until creamy. Gradually beat in the eggs, a little at a time, adding a little of the flour if the mixture starts to curdle.

2 Sift the flour with the spice and stir into the mixture. Add the ginger, dried fruit and almonds and stir the ingredients until they are evenly combined.

3 Turn the mixture into the prepared tin (see page 19) and level the surface. Bake in a preheated oven, 140°C (275°F), Gas Mark 1, for the time indicated in the chart or until a skewer, inserted into the centre, comes out clean. Leave to cool in the tin.

4 Remove the cake from the tin and wrap it in foil. If necessary, you can store it for up to 6 months in a cool, dry place until you are ready to ice it.

swiss roll

serves 10
cooking time 10–12 minutes

ingredients

3 large eggs
100 g (3½ oz) caster sugar,
  plus extra for dusting
100 g (3½ oz) self-raising flour
6–8 tablespoons raspberry
  or strawberry jam

1 Grease and line a Swiss roll tin, 33 x 23 cm (13 x 9 inches). Put the eggs and sugar in a heatproof bowl over a pan of gently simmering water and whisk until light and airy and the whisk leaves a trail when lifted. Remove from the heat and whisk for a further 3 minutes.

2 Sift the flour over the bowl and use a large metal spoon to fold it in, adding 1 tablespoon of hot water once most of the flour is incorporated. Turn the mixture into the tin and spread it into the corners. Bake in a preheated oven, 200°C (400°F), Gas Mark 6, for 10–12 minutes until just firm to the touch.

3 Meanwhile, sprinkle a sheet of greaseproof paper with caster sugar. Turn the warm cake out on to the paper and spread it with the jam. Starting from a short end, roll up the sponge. Place it seam-side down on a wire rack to cool.

chocolate swiss roll

serves 10
cooking time 10–12 minutes

ingredients

3 large eggs
75 g (3 oz) caster sugar,
  plus extra for dusting
50 g (2 oz) self-raising flour
25 g (1 oz) cocoa powder, sieved
300 ml (½ pint) double cream
  or 6–8 tablespoons jam

1 Make the cake as above, adding the cocoa powder with the flour in step 2.

2 Spread the warm cake with jam or with whipped cream before rolling it up.

fairy cakes

makes 12
cooking time 18–20 minutes

ingredients

150 g (5 oz) unsalted butter, softened
150 g (5 oz) caster sugar
175 g (6 oz) self-raising flour
3 eggs
2 teaspoons vanilla extract

1 Line a 12-section muffin tray with paper cake cases. Put all the ingredients in a bowl and beat with a hand-held electric whisk for 1–2 minutes until the mixture is light and creamy. Divide the mixture among the cases.

2 Bake the cakes in a preheated oven, 180°C (350°F), Gas Mark 4, for 18–20 minutes until they are risen and just firm to the touch. Transfer the cakes to a wire rack to cool.

choux pastry buns

makes 40

cooking time 23–25 minutes

ingredients

125 g (4 oz) plain flour
100 g (3½ oz) unsalted butter,
   cut into pieces
4 eggs, beaten

1 Sift the flour on to a piece of paper. Melt the butter in a medium saucepan with 300 ml (½ pint) water. Bring to the boil and tip the flour into the saucepan. Beat with a wooden spoon over the heat for about 1 minute or until the mixture forms a ball in the centre of the pan. Leave to cool for 2 minutes.

2 Gradually beat in the eggs, a little at a time, until the paste is smooth and glossy. Using 2 teaspoons, place spoonfuls of the paste on baking sheets, spacing them about 5 cm (2 inches) apart. You should have enough mixture for about 40 small spoonfuls.

3 Bake the buns in a preheated oven, 220°C (425°F), Gas Mark 7, for about 20 minutes until they are risen and golden. Remove from the oven and make a slit in the side of each bun to allow the steam to escape. Return them to the oven for a further 3–5 minutes until firm. Transfer to a wire rack to cool.

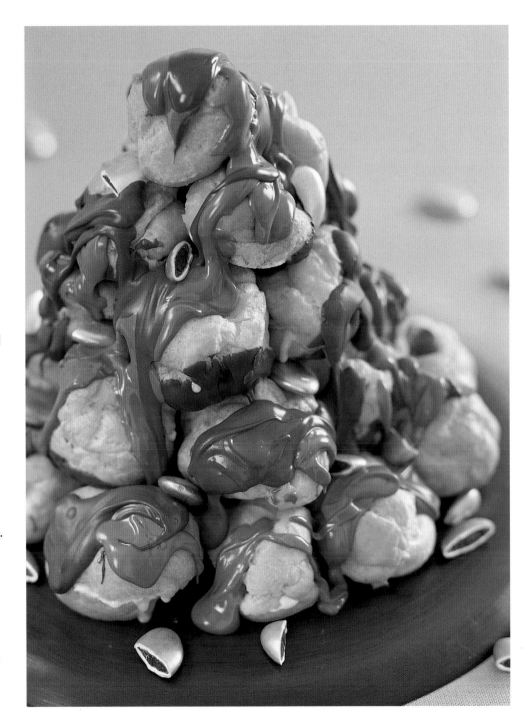

the icing on the cake

Many people find that icing and decorating their cakes is the most enjoyable part. There are so many options available that it really depends on the type of cake you've prepared and the nature of the celebration as to which type of icing you choose. The recipes in this book require many different kinds of icing – this section shows some of the most widely used.

buttercream

quantity	single	double	triple	quadruple
butter, softened	75 g (3 oz)	150 g (5 oz)	250 g (8 oz)	300 g (10 oz)
icing sugar	125 g (4 oz)	250 g (8 oz)	375 g (12 oz)	500 g (1 lb)
hot water	1 teaspoon	2 teaspoons	3 teaspoons	4 teaspoons
flavour variations				
vanilla extract	½ teaspoon	1 teaspoon	1½ teaspoons	2 teaspoons
citrus rind (use fruit juice instead of hot water)	2 teaspoons	4 teaspoons	6 teaspoons	8 teaspoons
coffee granules dissolved in hot water	1 teaspoon in 1 teaspoon water	2 teaspoons in 1 tablespoon water	3 teaspoons in 1 tablespoon water	4 teaspoons in 2 tablespoons water

Buttercream (or butter icing), which is simply made by blending together icing sugar and butter, has a delicious flavour and excellent texture, and it is extremely versatile. For the best flavour use a good quality, unsalted butter and beat it thoroughly with the icing sugar so it's easy to apply. Spread the cake with a thin layer of the buttercream to stick the crumbs in place, which will make a manageable base for the rest of the buttercream. Freshly packed icing sugar is usually fine to use straight from the pack, but if you open it and it looks a bit lumpy,

sift it first. If you want to flavour your buttercream, choose from one of the flavourings above and beat the ingredients into the buttercream once it's made. Remember that coffee will alter the colour of the buttercream, so bear this in mind if you're using it as a covering rather than as a filling.

1 Beat together the butter and a little of the icing sugar in a bowl until smooth.

2 Gradually beat in the remaining icing sugar and hot water until pale and creamy.

Glacé icing

Basic glacé icing is made by beating together icing sugar and water into a smooth paste. It really is that easy, but you'll probably want a little practice before you move on to variations. There are lots of alternative recipes that you can try, either to incorporate the flavours of the cake or to add subtle variations. For example, you can use orange or lemon juice instead of water or add other flavourings such as instant coffee or chocolate powder. If you want to include some colour in your icing, add a dash of food colouring. Use a thin glacé icing to coat the top of cakes, or you can add extra icing sugar for a stiffer consistency and then use this for decorative piping.

Rolled fondant

This is a ready-to-use commercial icing that's available from larger supermarkets or specialist cake shops. It generally comes in white but, like the other icings, you can easily adapt the colour and flavour to suit your needs by kneading it with food colouring or flavouring extracts. Fondant is extremely adaptable and you can either roll it out and cut it into shapes or use it to create novelty decorations to put on top of cakes. Rolled fondant has to be kneaded before use to warm it up and make it more pliable. Dust your work surface with icing sugar when you're working with the fondant to stop it sticking – otherwise it can be very messy to work with.

Writing icing

This is another ready-to-use commercial icing that comes in tubes with a variety of tips for piping. It's also available in a range of different colours. It's great for birthday cakes in particular because you can easily write names and ages on top of your cake.

Ganache

Ganache is one of the most luxurious of all the icings, a pure blend of chocolate and cream. Once made, it'll need 15–30 minutes to thicken up before use, but keep an eye on it because it will gradually become too thick to use so you need to be ready when it's exactly the right consistency. This quantity makes enough to cover a 20 cm (8 inch) round cake.

dark chocolate ganache

makes enough to cover a 20 cm (8 inch) round cake

ingredients

    300 ml (½ pint) double cream
    300 g (10 oz) good quality dark
      chocolate, chopped

1 Heat the cream in a medium, heavy-based saucepan until it is bubbling around the edge. Remove from the heat and stir in the chopped chocolate.

2 Leave to stand until the chocolate has melted. Turn the mixture into a bowl and chill until the ganache is cool enough to hold its shape. The cooling time will depend on the temperature to which the cream is heated. As a guide, check after about 15 minutes, although it might take 30–40 minutes.

white chocolate ganache

makes enough to cover a 20 cm (8 inch) round cake

ingredients

    300 ml (½ pint) double cream
    300 g (10 oz) good quality white
      chocolate, chopped

1 Heat half the cream in a medium, heavy-based saucepan until it is bubbling around the edge. Remove from the heat and stir in the chocolate.

2 Leave to stand until the chocolate has melted. Turn the mixture into a bowl and chill for about 15 minutes until cold.

3 Stir in the remaining cream and whisk with a hand-held electric whisk until the ganache just holds its shape. Don't over-whisk the mixture or the cream will start to curdle.

chocolate fudge icing

This icing develops a fudge-like consistency when set, making a delicious filling and covering for chocolate or sponge cakes. It thickens as it cools, so make sure you use it while it is spreadable. If it does solidify before you've had a chance to use it, simply beat in a dash of hot water. It's an easy recipe to double up on quantities if you've made a larger cake.

makes enough to cover a 20 cm (8 inch) round cake

ingredients
25 g (1 oz) unsalted butter
15 g (½ oz) cocoa powder
175 g (6 oz) icing sugar
2 tablespoons milk

1 Melt the butter in a small saucepan. Stir in the cocoa powder and cook, stirring constantly, for 30 seconds until smooth. Remove the pan from the heat and gradually stir in the icing sugar (no need to sift) and milk, mixing until smooth.

2 Return the pan to the heat for 1 minute, stirring constantly, until the icing has a glossy pouring consistency. Quickly spread the icing over the cake while it is still warm.

royal icing

Royal icing hardens once it dries out. To compensate for this, if you're making a wedding or Christmas cake well in advance, beat in a teaspoon of glycerine. If you're not using the icing immediately, press a sheet of clingfilm directly over the surface of the icing to prevent a crust forming.

makes enough to cover a 20 cm (8 inch) round cake

ingredients
2 egg whites
500 g (1 lb) icing sugar

1 Using a hand-held electric whisk, beat the egg whites in a large bowl with a little of the icing sugar until smooth.

2 Gradually whisk in the remaining icing sugar until the icing is softly peaking. You might not need all the icing sugar.

techniques and tips

There are a number of techniques that are good to know if you're planning to make a lot of party cakes. You'll find all these useful for the recipes in this book.

Lining a round cake tin

Using the tin as a guide, draw a circle on greaseproof paper and cut it out. Cut strips of paper a little wider than the height of the tin, fold over a lip about 1 cm (½ inch) wide and snip it at intervals. Fit the paper around the sides of the tin so the lip sits flat on the base. If you need more than one strip of paper to go round the sides, overlap them slightly. Press the circle into the base and brush all the paper with melted butter or margarine.

Lining a square cake tin

This technique is similar to the one above, but once you've cut the square base and strips, you only need to make snips in the paper at the corners to make sure it fits squarely into the corners of the tin. Brush the paper with a little melted butter or margarine. For shallower tins, such as roasting tins, simply snip into the corners of a large piece of greased greaseproof paper and press it into the base of the tin.

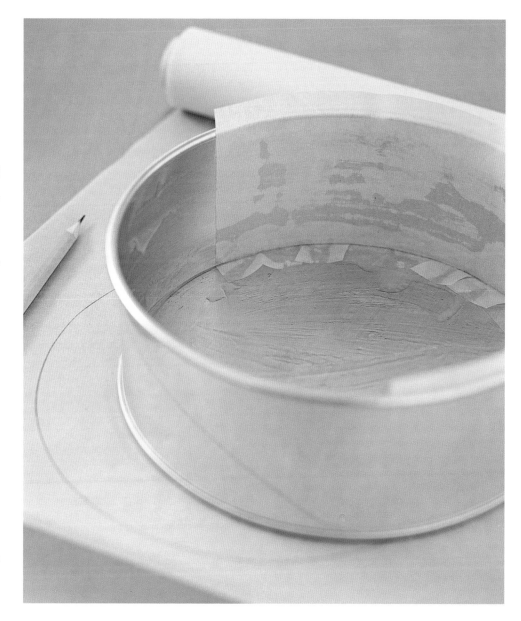

Using ready-to-roll icing

Soft and pliable, shop-bought, ready-to-roll icing is easy to use. Large packs of white icing are widely available, and many large supermarkets sell smaller packs of icings in basic colours. For a choice of more interesting colours try your local cake-decorating shop, where you should find a good range of different shades in handy 250 g (8 oz) packs. Once the pack is opened, the icing will gradually dry out, making it impossible to use. To prevent this, tightly wrap any unused icing in clingfilm, even if it's just for a short time. Leftover icing can be stored in a cool place for several months or in the freezer. Before using, knead it with a bit of icing sugar to remove any stickiness.

Food colourings

Food colourings are available in several forms. Liquid colours – the type often available in supermarkets – tend to be less intense, so you might not be able to reach the shade you want before the icing has become too wet to use. They are useful for pastel shades, however, or for painting on to icing.

Paste colours are much more intense and come in a wider range of colours. Basic ones, including red and black, can be bought from most supermarkets, but for a much wider choice, visit a specialist cake-decorating shop.

Powder colours, also available from cake-decorating shops, can be kneaded into icing

but they're usually just dusted on to icing, once the icing is shaped and set. Gold and silver food colours are available in liquid form (just give them a stir before use) or as a powder, which can be mixed to a 'paint' with a dash of flavourless cooking oil or a drop of vodka. Some metallic colours aren't edible and should therefore not be applied directly to the cake.

Colouring white icing

Dust your work surface with icing sugar or cornflour and lightly knead the icing to soften it. Use the tip of a cocktail stick to dot the icing with paste colouring. A little paste colour goes a long way, so add it sparingly at first, particularly if you want a pastel shade. You can always add more later but it's too late if you add too much. If you're adding liquid colour use a cocktail stick or the handle of a teaspoon. Knead the icing until the colour is evenly distributed. For a marbled effect, leave the icing streaked with colour.

Covering a cake board with icing

Cakes look more sophisticated if you cover the cake board with icing. This can be done either once the cake is iced on the board and only the edges show or, if a lot of the board shows, before the cake is positioned. To cover the whole board, brush the surface of the

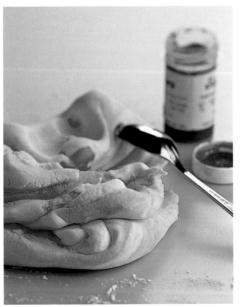

board with water. Thinly roll out the icing on a surface dusted with icing sugar or cornflour and lift it over the board. Smooth the icing with the palms of your hands and use a sharp knife to trim off the excess paste around the edges.

To cover the edges of the board, brush the top edge of the board lightly with water. Roll out long, thin strips of the icing trimmings and lay them around the cake, butting a neat cut edge against the cake. Smooth down and trim off the excess around the edges of the board. For a square cake, it's easiest to cover one side of the board at a time. For a round cake, work with the longest strip you can manage, to avoid having too many joins.

Covering a cake with ready-to-roll icing

Use a palette knife to spread the top and sides of the cake with a thin layer of smooth apricot or red fruit jam or buttercream. Lightly knead the icing on a surface dusted with icing sugar to soften it slightly and roll it out to a round or square that is about 12 cm (5 inches) larger in diameter than the cake. Lift the icing over a rolling pin and drape it over the cake. Smooth the icing over the top of the cake and ease it to fit around the sides. Because icing is so pliable you should be able to shape it around the sides without leaving any creases. Trim off the excess icing. Using the palms of your hands dusted with icing sugar, smooth out any bumps, making the surface as smooth and flat as possible.

Covering a cake with almond paste

Rich fruit cakes are usually covered with a layer of almond paste before being iced. Use

exactly the same technique as for covering a cake with ready-to-roll icing. Spread the cake with apricot jam and then add the almond paste. There's no need to let the almond paste dry out before covering it with either ready-to-roll or royal icing.

quantities of almond paste

Square cake	Round cake	Almond paste
12 cm (5 inch)	15 cm (6 inch)	400 g (13 oz)
18 cm (7 inch)	20 cm (8 inch)	750 g (1½ lb)
23 cm (9 inch)	25 cm (10 inch)	1.25 kg (2½ lb)

the finishing touches

This is where a homemade cake really comes into its own. The final decorations will distinguish a wedding cake from a birthday cake and will help to give your cake that personal touch. As tempting as it is, don't overdo the decorations – often the simplest cakes are the most appealing and you don't want to ruin all your hard work by cramming on too many different colours and shapes.

Icing shapes

Ready-to-roll icing is easy to use, which makes it perfect for cutting out a variety of shapes. You can either place these directly on the cake or set them aside on a baking sheet lined with greaseproof paper or nonstick baking paper until they have set hard. Roll out the icing thinly on a surface dusted with icing sugar and cut out the shapes. Dip the cutter or knife in icing sugar first so that it doesn't stick to the icing.

Piped icing

You'll find a variety of tubes of icing in larger supermarkets or cake shops, but you can make your own paper piping bag if you prefer. Cut out a 25 cm (10 inch) square of greaseproof paper or nonstick baking paper and fold the paper diagonally in half to make a triangle. Cut along the folded line. Holding the centre of the long edge towards you, curl the right-hand point of the triangle over to meet the centre point, forming a cone. Bring the left-hand point over the cone so the 3 points meet. Fold the paper over several times at the points to stop the paper unravelling. Half-fill the bag with your chosen icing and fold up the open end to secure the bag before snipping off the tip. Begin by snipping off a tiny amount to see how finely the mixture flows out. You can then easily snip off a bit more for a wider line of piping if necessary.

Chocolate curls

Run a vegetable peeler along the edge of a bar of chocolate to make curls. These make a simple but attractive decoration for any number of party cakes and can either be scattered over the cake or else clustered in the centre.

Flowers

Fresh flowers look absolutely gorgeous on a cake and are often sufficient in terms of decoration. Add them at the last minute so they remain fresh for as long as possible, or you can wrap the ends of the stems in damp cotton wool and then clingfilm. Alternatively, you could try using dried or artificial flowers, although fresh flowers will always look much more effective.

Sweets

It's a good idea to keep an eye out for any interesting shaped sweets when you're out shopping. You can then tuck them away in the cupboard until you're baking your next party cake and use them to add an interesting and different twist to the final look of your decorated cake.

Painted decorations

If you like painting and have a steady hand, you'll find painting decorations on the cake with food colouring and a fine artist's paintbrush really rewarding and effective. If there's time, let the icing set first so that it won't dent if you rest your hand on it for support.

1
kids' cakes

ballet shoes

serves 8–10

decoration time 25 minutes

2 x 23 cm (9 inch) bought or
homemade chocolate Swiss Rolls
(see page 12)
3 tablespoons smooth apricot jam
icing sugar or cornflour, for dusting
500 g (1 lb) pink ready-to-roll icing
75 g (3 oz) white ready-to-roll icing
pink piping icing or jam
1.5 metres (5 feet) pink satin ribbon

1 Use a serrated knife to trim the ends of the Swiss rolls into a curve. Scoop an oval, about 14 x 5 cm (5½ x 2 inches) and 2 cm (¾ inch) deep, out of the top of each cake. Brush away any loose crumbs and spread the cakes with the apricot jam.

2 Dust your work surface with icing sugar or cornflour and roll out half the pink icing so that it is at least 5 cm (2 inches) larger than a cake all the way around. Lift the icing over the rolling pin and drape it over one of the cakes. Ease it over the sides, smoothing it with your fingertips dusted with cornflour. Trim off the excess and wrap the trimmings in clingfilm. Transfer the iced cake to a baking sheet lined with nonstick baking paper. Cover the second cake in the same way with the remaining pink icing and transfer it to the baking sheet.

3 Knead 25 g (1 oz) of the pink icing trimmings with the white icing, then cut it in half. Roll out one piece to a 15 x 6 cm (6 x 2½ inch) oval. Press the oval into one ballet shoe and trim off the excess. Repeat with the remaining icing and the other shoe. Cut thin strips from the trimmings and shape them into bows. Transfer the bows to the baking sheet to dry.

4 Shape the remaining pink icing into a long rope, then flatten it with a rolling pin to 30 cm (12 inches) long. Cut the strip in half lengthways and trim the outer edges with a fluted pastry wheel. Brush the top edges of the ballet shoes with water and press the strips around the join where the pale and darker pink icings meet. Add the icing bows, sticking them in place with a little piping icing or jam.

5 Leave the cakes to dry, if you have time, then arrange them in a box lined with patterned tissue paper or on an oval cake board covered with a thin layer of white ready-to-roll icing. Decorate with pink satin ribbons.

quick tips

- If you are short of time, put the covered cakes straight on to a cake board and decorate them immediately.

- If you cannot find pink ready-to-roll icing you can adapt white icing to suit your needs. Just add drops of red food colouring, a little at a time, until it is the desired shade.

rapunzel

serves 12

decoration time 30 minutes

double quantity pale green Buttercream (see page 15)

28 cm (11 inch) round cake board

3 x 15 cm (6 inch) bought chocolate Swiss rolls

2 bought chocolate mini-Swiss rolls

icing sugar or cornflour, for dusting

750 g (1½ lb) white ready-to-roll icing

red paste food colouring

75 g (3 oz) mini-marshmallows

1 tube each yellow, black and red writing icing

50 g (2 oz) yellow ready-to-roll icing

1 white chocolate button

1 pink wafer biscuit

sugar flowers

candles and candle-holders

1 Thickly spread the buttercream over the cake board. Cut 5 cm (2 inches) off one of the large Swiss rolls and stick the cut-off slice on to the top of the second Swiss roll with a little buttercream. Thinly spread buttercream over the sides and ends of all the Swiss rolls and mini-rolls.

2 Dust your work surface with icing sugar or cornflour and knead the white ready-to-roll icing. Add a little red colouring and knead again until partially mixed, to give a marbled effect. Roll out the icing and cut out rectangles, 20 cm (8 inches) wide and the same length as each roll, to cover all the Swiss rolls. Cover the larger Swiss roll first and re-roll the trimmings as required.

3 Put the cakes on the board, standing them close together on their ends. Position the mini-rolls at the front with a gap between them for the castle entrance. Roll out the remaining pink icing trimmings and cut out a 5 cm (2 inch) square. Cut a castellated design along one edge, then stick the gate to the mini-rolls with a little buttercream.

4 Decorate the tops of the towers with mini-marshmallows stuck in place with yellow writing icing. Add a few marshmallows around the base.

5 Make Rapunzel. Knead the yellow ready-to-roll icing and press a small ball into a round. Add the white chocolate button for the face and fold yellow icing hair around the head. Cut the remaining icing in half and shape each piece into 2 long ropes. Twist them together and stick them to the side of the tallest tower with yellow writing icing. Draw Rapunzel's eyes and mouth with black and red writing icing and stick the head in position. Add tiny pieces of icing at the end of the 'plait' to suggest 3 strands.

6 Make the window. Cut the wafer biscuit in half and cut a small piece off each end. Stick the larger window pieces to the tower either side of Rapunzel's head and stick one of the shorter pieces of biscuit on the castle entrance to make a drawbridge. Add sugar flowers to the cake board and candles in holders to the top of the turrets.

quick tip

• If the castle's entrance droops slightly, prop it up with a piece of folded foil. Remove the foil just before serving.

dolls' house

serves 20

decoration time 30 minutes

5 x 350 g (11½ oz) bought chocolate
marble loaf cakes

30 cm (12 inch) round cake board,
plain or iced

quadruple quantity pink Buttercream
(see page 15)

18 pale pink rectangular iced biscuits

100 g (3½ oz) midget gems or other
small fruit gums

200 g (7 oz) jelly beans

9 pale yellow rectangular
iced biscuits

4 pieces pale green fruit rock

1 tube yellow writing icing

selection of icing flowers

white chocolate buttons

1 Trim the tops and a little off the sides of 4 of the cakes so that they stack together closely on the cake board to make a block 2 cakes wide and 2 cakes high. Sandwich the cakes together with buttercream, then spread a little more on the top. Cut the last cake in half diagonally and butt the halves together to make the roof.

2 Cover the sides and roof of the house thickly with buttercream. Arrange the pink biscuits to make the overlapping roof tiles. Arrange the midget gems or fruit gums along the ridge of the roof. Stick the jelly beans under the eaves, down the edges of the house and around the bottom on the cake board.

3 Stick 2 yellow biscuits to each side of the house to make windows and another for a door at one end. Use a serrated knife to cut the fruit rock in half and press the pieces on to the cake under the windows. Pipe on window bars with yellow icing, then pipe on dots of icing and stick the flowers in place. Attach a midget gem or fruit gum doorknob.

4 Add a few extra flowers to the cake board and use white chocolate buttons to make a path to the front door.

quick tips

- Cover the cake board with 250 g (8 oz) ready-to-roll pale green icing, sticking down the edges with a little apricot jam. Trim the edges of the icing and leave to harden before placing the cake on top.

- Make an all-chocolate version with white Chocolate Fudge Icing (see page 18) or vanilla Buttercream (see page 15) with chocolate-covered biscuits and sweets for decorations.

it's my birthday

serves 6

decoration time 30 minutes

18 cm (7 inch) round bought or homemade Basic Sponge Cake (see page 9)

20 cm (8 inch) square cake board

double quantity pink Buttercream (see page 15)

4 tablespoons strawberry jam

icing sugar or cornflour, for dusting

500 g (1 lb) white ready-to-roll icing

1 tube white piping icing

2 x 6 cm (2½ inch) thick, non-drip white or pink candles

20 g (¾ oz) pack of sugar flowers

1 Using the cake tin as a guide, cut a circle of paper the same size as the sponge cake layers. Fold it into a wedge shape, retaining the curved edge. Using the folded paper as a guide, cut the cake layers into wedge shapes. Piece the trimmings together on the folded paper, trimming again where necessary, to make a third wedge.

2 Put one wedge on the cake board and spread it thickly with buttercream so that the icing protrudes slightly over the edge. Dot with half the jam, again adding some near the edges of the cake. Cover with the separate pieces of cake and spread with buttercream and jam as before, then top with the third wedge.

3 Spread the top and rounded side of the cake with a thin layer of buttercream. Dust your work surface with icing sugar or cornflour and knead and roll out the white ready-to-roll icing to make a triangle, 28 x 25 cm (11 x 10 inches). Drape the icing over the cake, smoothing it into place with your fingertips dusted with a little icing sugar or cornflour.

4 Trim the icing to the exact shape of the cake. Brush any crumbs off the trimmings, knead again and re-roll. Cut moon shapes, about 10 cm (4 inches) long, to make swags. Curl up the long edges and drape them around the side of the cake, securing them with white piping icing.

5 Use a large star tube to pipe rosettes of pink buttercream between the swags and around the top and bottom edges of the cake. Decorate the cake with the sugar flowers. Pipe larger rosettes on top of the cake and press a candle into the centre of each.

quick tips

- Cover the cake and board with a plastic cake dome or a large upturned bowl so that the cut edges do not dry out. Do not use clingfilm or foil in case you damage the soft buttercream.

- For a more contemporary look, use different coloured icing and replace the flowers with jelly diamonds or other sweets.

three naughty kittens

serves 4

decoration time 30 minutes

8 bought or homemade Fairy Cakes
(see page 13)

single quantity red Buttercream
(see page 15)

200 g (7 oz) strawberry-flavoured
bootlaces

20 cm (8 inch) round silver
cake board

icing sugar or cornflour, for dusting

250 g (8 oz) black ready-to-roll icing

75 g (3 oz) white ready-to-roll icing

6 edible metallic balls

1 tube black writing icing

1 If necessary trim the tops of the cakes to level them. Spread a little buttercream over the cake tops and sandwich them together in pairs. Spread buttercream thinly all over the tops and sides of the cakes.

2 Wrap the strawberry bootlaces around the cakes so that the buttercream is completely covered until they resemble balls of wool. Reserve a few spare strands. Arrange the 'balls of wool' on the cake board and twist the remaining bootlaces between them.

3 Make the kittens. Dust your fingers with icing sugar or cornflour and use the black icing to mould an oval, 3.5 cm (1½ inches) long. Put it on top of, or at the base of, a cake and add a small head about 1.5 cm (¾ inch) in diameter. Shape 4 small legs and a tail and press them on to the body. Make ears with tiny balls of white icing wrapped in black and press them on to the kitten. Press on edible metallic balls for eyes. Add tiny ropes of white for whiskers and stick them on with dots of black writing icing. Add tiny balls of white for paws.

4 Repeat to make a second seated black kitten in the same way, but add a circle of white icing to the tummy. Knead the remaining black and white icing together, shape into a tabby cat and arrange on a ball of wool.

quick tips

• If you like, make an extra kitten so that each child has one to keep or eat.

• If you are short of time, buy little plastic cats from a toy or cake-decorating shop.

• A large ball of wool could be made with 2 cakes made the old-fashioned way in pudding basins.

paint box

serves 6

decoration time 20 minutes

18 cm (7 inch) square bought or homemade Basic Sponge Cake (see page 9) or bought angel cake

20 cm (8 inch) square silver cake board

2 tablespoons smooth apricot jam

icing sugar or cornflour, for dusting

200 g (7 oz) white ready-to-roll icing

125 g (4 oz) red ready-to-roll icing

black paste food colouring

5 different coloured clear fruit sweets or jelly sweets

selection of crayon candles

1 Cut the cake in half lengthways and put both pieces, with the long edges touching, on the cake board at a slight angle. Spread the top and sides of each half with jam.

2 Dust your work surface with icing sugar or cornflour and knead and roll out three-quarters of the white icing. Wrap the remaining icing in clingfilm.

3 Drape the rolled-out icing over the cakes, forming a ridge around the edge and making a cavity for the brush holder and paints. Smooth over the sides and trim off the excess. Knead any trimmings again.

4 Reserve half the red icing to make the paintbrush. Knead and shape the remainder into a rope long enough to go around the base and lid. Flatten it with a rolling pin and cut it into a thin strip with a pastry wheel. Stick it around the edge of the paint box with water.

5 Shape the reserved red icing into a paintbrush handle. Use some of the white trimmings to make the ferrule. Colour a little of the remaining white icing black and roll it into a strip. Make a series of cuts almost down to the base, like a fringe, then roll it up for brush bristles. Press the bristles on to the ferrule. Position the brush in the paint box and arrange the sweets to resemble paints.

6 Insert the appropriate number of crayon candles into balls of white icing and stick them on to the cake board. Arrange the remaining candles on the lid of the paint box.

quick tips

- For young children use soft jelly sweets rather than hard boiled sweets.

- Although the cake may be made several days in advance, don't add the sweets until just before the party because they will begin to dissolve after a few hours.

snakes and ladders

serves 12

decoration time 25 minutes

3 bought Battenberg cakes

25 cm (10 inch) square cake board

1 tablespoon smooth apricot jam

2 lattice-shaped chocolate bars

icing sugar or cornflour, for dusting

200 g (7 oz) white ready-to-roll icing

red, yellow and green paste food colourings

1 tube red writing icing

1 tube yellow writing icing

edible silver balls

6 different-coloured covered chocolate drops

candles and candle-holders

1 Cut the marzipan covering from the cakes and reserve it. Thickly slice the cakes and put the pieces close together on the cake board, arranging them so that the colours alternate to give a chequerboard effect.

2 Cut the reserved marzipan into strips the same thickness as the cake. Brush the edges of the cake with jam and cover the sides with the marzipan strips.

3 Unwrap the chocolate bars, cut them into different lengths and arrange the pieces at angles on the cake to make ladders.

4 Dust your work surface with icing sugar or cornflour. Knead a small piece of white ready-to-roll icing, colour it red and roll it into a ball. Cut it into a cube to make a die. Cut the remaining icing in half. Colour half of it orange with a little red and yellow colouring, and the rest green. Shape a cube of green icing for the second die in the same way as the red one and set aside.

5 Roll some of the remaining green icing into a rope, shape it into a small snake and lift it on to the cake. Make a second, larger orange snake and then an orange and green snake by twisting 2 ropes of coloured icing together and curving them into a snake shape. Roll out the green trimmings and use them to make a small arrow. Position the arrow on the bottom left-hand corner to mark the start of the game.

6 Decorate the snakes with zigzag lines of red and yellow writing icing. Stick silver balls on the snakes with a little yellow icing to represent eyes. Arrange the coloured sweet counters on the cake. Complete with candles to mark the end of the game.

quick tip

- If you can't get lattice-shaped chocolate bars use chocolate sticks for the ladders, with smaller pieces for rungs. Alternatively, you can make the ladders with strips of brown ready-to-roll icing.

funny clown

serves 8

decoration time 20 minutes

18 cm (7 inch) round bought or
homemade Basic Sponge Cake
(see page 9)

single quantity vanilla Buttercream
(see page 15)

23 cm (9 inch) round cake board

icing sugar or cornflour, for dusting

500 g (1 lb) white ready-to-roll icing

125 g (4 oz) red ready-to-roll icing

125 g (4 oz) blue ready-to-roll icing

1 yellow and black liquorice sweet

100 g (3½ oz) apple- or strawberry-
flavoured bootlaces

1 tube green or red writing icing

1 Sandwich the 2 halves of the cake together with a thick layer of buttercream. Put them on the cake board and spread the top and sides of the cake and the rim of the board thinly with buttercream. Reserve the remaining buttercream.

2 Dust your work surface with icing sugar or cornflour and knead the white ready-to-roll icing. Roll it out until it is large enough to cover the entire cake and rim of the board. Drape the icing over the rolling pin to lift it and smooth it over the cake with your fingertips dusted with icing sugar or cornflour. Press it over the cake board so that it is firmly in place and trim off the excess.

3 Form the red ready-to-roll icing shape a ball for the clown's nose and a rope about 12 cm (5 inches) long. Curve the rope and flatten it with a rolling pin for the mouth. Transfer the nose and mouth to the top of the cake, sticking them in place with a little of the remaining buttercream.

4 Knead the blue ready-to-roll icing, roll it out thinly and cut out a rectangle, 28 x 6 cm (11 x 2½ inches). Put this on the base of the cake in a wavy line, sticking it in place with dots of buttercream. Re-roll the trimmings and cut 2 eyes and a thin strip for the centre of the mouth. Press these on to the cake.

5 Halve the liquorice sweet and stick it on to the cake for eyeballs. Make the bootlaces curly by wrapping them around the handle of a wooden spoon or metal skewer, hold for 1–2 minutes, then slide off and stick to the cake with writing icing for the clown's hair.

quick tips

- If you can't buy ready-coloured ready-to-roll icing, colour your own icing with paste food colouring, but remember that liquid colours do not give the same intensity and too much will make the icing sticky and watery.

- If your children don't like liquorice, make the eyeballs with 2 small balls of white icing.

pirate ship

serves 16

decoration time 30 minutes

4 x 300 g (10 oz) bought double
chocolate loaf cakes

35 x 20 cm (14 x 8 inch) silver
cake board

double quantity chocolate
Buttercream (see page 15)

300 g (10 oz) chocolate
finger biscuits

8 giant covered chocolate drops

7 long wooden skewers

raffia or fine string

selection of orange, green and
black paper

selection of small plastic
pirate figures

shredded blue tissue paper

1 If necessary level the tops of the cakes. Put 2 cakes on the cake board and sandwich the 2 shortest sides together with a little buttercream. Cut one-third off one of the cakes. Spread the top of the cakes with buttercream and stick the other 2 cakes on top with the small slice in the centre so that the second layer extends over the first. Cut one end to a point for the prow of the ship and put one of the off-cuts underneath to support it.

2 Spread the remaining buttercream over the top and sides of the cake, then stick chocolate fingers over both sides. Add chocolate drops for portholes.

3 Make the masts. Tie 2 skewers into a cross with a little raffia or string, trimming the sticks if necessary. Repeat to make 2 more. Cut rectangles of paper for sails, make holes along the top edge with a hole punch and lace to the masts with raffia or fine string. Add a hole to the centre base of the sails and tie down to the masts. Add a triangular sail to a single stick. Cut a black flag and tape it to the top of one of the masts. Insert the masts into the cake.

4 Complete the cake with plastic pirate figures. Arrange pieces of tissue paper on the cake board to represent the sea.

quick tips

- If you cannot find chocolate loaf cakes the same size as required in the recipe, buy whatever is available and increase or reduce the quantity of icing and the number of finger biscuits accordingly. Some loaf cakes have steep domes, so level the tops before using.

- If you prefer, you can cover the cake board with a sea of blue buttercream or desiccated coconut, coloured blue and held in place with a little jam.

full steam ahead

serves 8

decoration time 30 minutes

2 x 300 g (10 oz) bought chocolate marble cakes

28 x 5 cm (11 x 2 inch) silver cake board

4 tablespoons smooth apricot jam

500 g (1 lb) red ready-to-roll icing

icing sugar or cornflour, for dusting

15 cm (6 inch) bought jam or chocolate Swiss roll, cut in half

75 g (3 oz) yellow ready-to-roll icing

8 round jam-filled or iced ring biscuits

1 tube red writing icing

2 large red jelly sweets

2 large yellow jelly sweets

200 g (7 oz) coloured jelly beans

1 candle and candle-holder

1 If necessary trim the tops of the cakes to level them. Put one cake near the end of the cake board. Cut one-third off the remaining cake for the cab and use the remaining piece for the tender. Spread the top and sides of all the cakes with jam.

2 Reserve one-third of the red icing and wrap it in clingfilm. Dust your work surface with icing sugar or cornflour and knead the remaining red icing. Roll out just over half and use it to cover the engine base. Smooth the surface and trim off the excess. Re-roll the trimmings and amalgamate them with the remaining kneaded icing. Use it to cover the cab sides and the Swiss roll boiler, leaving the ends of the Swiss roll uncovered. Put the cab and boiler in position, securing them with jam if necessary. If the cab seems a little wobbly, insert a wooden skewer or plastic straw through the cab into the base.

3 Cover the tender in the same way with the reserved red icing, folding the edges of the icing over the top edge of the cake. Put the tender on the cake board behind the engine.

4 Roll out the yellow icing and use it to cover the cab top, to add rectangular windows and to cover the end of the Swiss roll boiler.

5 Stick the biscuits to the sides of the engine with red writing icing. Add jelly sweets to represent buffers and lights, sticking them in place with red writing icing. Pipe a number on front of the boiler. Fill the tender with sweets and complete the engine with a candle and candle-holder.

quick tips

- If you are having lots of children to a party add extra trucks of sweets, made in the same way as the tender, and arrange the cake on a long strip of cardboard or a thin piece of wood covered with foil or paper. You could add a chocolate finger biscuit track with sugar crystals or demerara sugar for gravel.

- The tender could be filled with covered chocolate drops, jelly babies or chocolate buttons instead of jelly beans.

twelfth night crown

serves 8

decoration time 20 minutes

18 cm (7 inch) round bought or homemade Basic Sponge Cake (see page 9)

single quantity orange-flavoured Buttercream (see page 15)

23 cm (9 inch) round cake board

4 tablespoons sugar balls

icing sugar or cornflour, for dusting

500 g (1 lb) yellow ready-to-roll icing

16 black jelly beans

9 clear fruit sweets

1 tube yellow writing icing

1 Cut the cake in half horizontally and sandwich the layers together with some of the buttercream. Put them on the cake board and spread buttercream thinly over the sides of the cake and thickly over the top. Sprinkle sugar balls over the top.

2 Dust your work surface with icing sugar or cornflour. Knead and roll out the yellow ready-to-roll icing and trim it to a rectangle, 60 x 8 cm (24 x 3½ inches). Use a plain 6 cm (2½ inch) biscuit cutter to scallop the top edge, then carefully press the strip of icing around the edge of the cake.

3 Knead the trimmings and shape them into a rope, 60 cm (24 inches) long. Press the rope to the base of the cake, trimming the ends if necessary and sticking it in place with a little buttercream. Spread the remaining buttercream over the icing rope to resemble a fur trim. Decorate with black jelly beans.

4 Stick the clear fruit sweets on to the crown for jewels, using a generous quantity of writing icing to hold them in place.

quick tips

• You could cover the top of the cake with rumpled red or blue ready-to-roll icing to give the impression of velvet.

• Don't add the clear fruit sweets until the last moment because they might dissolve if left to stand for any length of time. You need to be quite generous with the writing icing or you will find that the sweets slide off the crown.

penguins' igloo

serves 8

decoration time 30 minutes

3 tablespoons smooth apricot jam

2 x 15 cm (6 inch) round bought or
homemade filled Basic Sponge Cakes
(see page 9)

28 cm (11 inch) round cake board,
plain or iced

icing sugar or cornflour, for dusting

500 g (1 lb) white ready-to-roll icing

1 bought mini-Swiss roll

4 tablespoons desiccated coconut

250 g (8 oz) black ready-to-roll icing

25 g (1 oz) red ready-to-roll icing

14 edible silver balls

1 Spread a little jam over the top of one of the cakes and put the second cake on top. Use a small serrated knife to cut away the edges of the top cake to make a domed igloo shape. Spread the top and sides of the cakes with jam and put it on the cake board just off centre.

2 Dust your work surface with icing sugar or cornflour. Knead the white ready-to-roll icing and roll it out to a circle 25 cm (10 inches) across. Drape the icing over the cake and smooth it over the top and sides. Trim off the excess and knead the trimmings.

3 Cut the mini-Swiss roll in half and put one piece on top of the other, sticking it in place with jam. Roll out a little of the remaining white ready-to-roll icing and use it to cover the mini-Swiss roll, pressing a door shape in one end. Butt the mini-roll up against the igloo, sticking it in place with jam. Use a small knife to mark snow bricks all over the igloo and tunnel entrance.

4 Shape the remaining white icing into small balls and set them aside. Sprinkle coconut around the base of the igloo.

5 Make the penguins. Shape black ready-to-roll icing into 5 small balls and the same number of slightly larger balls. Press the small balls on top of the larger ones to make the penguins' heads and bodies. Roll the remaining black icing into 5 ropes, each about 5 cm (2 inches) long. Flatten the ropes with your fingertips, shaping the ends into points, and wrap them around the penguin bodies for wings. Add tiny triangles of red icing for beaks and silver balls for eyes.

6 Press 5 of the smaller white balls of icing into ovals and press them on to the penguins' tummies. Arrange the penguins on the cake and add the remaining small balls of white icing for snowballs.

quick tips

- If you make your own cakes you will need to make 2 pairs and fill them with buttercream or jam.

- Cover the cake board with 250 g (8 oz) blue ready-to-roll icing and stick it on to the cake board with a little smooth apricot jam, spread around the outer edges of the board.

the doyouthinkhesawus dinosaur

serves 10

decoration time 30 minutes

23 cm (9 inch) round bought or homemade Basic Sponge Cake (see page 9)

6 tablespoons smooth apricot jam

25 x 35 cm (10 x 14 inch) rectangular or 38 cm (15 inch) oval cake board

500 g (1 lb) white ready-to-roll icing

green, blue and yellow paste food colourings

icing sugar or cornflour, for dusting

250 g (8 oz) red ready-to-roll icing

50 g (2 oz) pack covered chocolate drops

1 tube yellow writing icing

sugar crystals

1 Cut a 4 cm (1½ inch) strip from the centre of the cake, then sandwich together the half-moon shapes with some of the jam. Stand the cake on the board so that the curved sides are uppermost. Halve the remaining strip of cake and use one half for the head, rounding off the corners to make the snout and back of the head. Use the other half for the tail, cutting a diagonal slice off the length of the tail piece. Turn it around and butt the pieces together to lengthen the tail. Brush the top and sides of the cake with apricot jam.

2 Knead the white icing to soften it, then mix in a little green colouring until it is evenly coloured. Add more green, blue and yellow colourings and knead briefly for a marbled effect. Dust your work surface with icing sugar or cornflour and roll out the icing until it is large enough to cover the dinosaur. Drape the icing over the cake, smooth the surface and trim off the excess. Cut a triangle for the end of the tail, shape legs, eyes and nostrils from the trimmings and stick them on to the cake with the remaining jam.

3 Knead the red icing. Shape small balls of the icing into triangles and press them along the top of the dinosaur for back spines. Roll out and cut a tongue and press it on the mouth.

4 Stick the sweets on the dinosaur's back and eye sockets with yellow writing icing, then pipe on eyeballs. Sprinkle sugar crystals on the board around the dinosaur.

quick tips

- The cake could be flavoured with a little grated orange rind and sandwiched together with one quantity of plain or orange-flavoured Buttercream (see page 15).

- Recycle old cake boards and cover marks or scratches with new foil or coloured ready-to-roll icing, sticking it in place with a little jam, or desiccated coconut.

three little pigs

serves 12

decoration time 30 minutes

1 bought triple variety pack or
3 square homemade flavoured Basic
Sponge Cakes (see page 9), each
275 g (9 oz)

30 x 25 cm (12 x 10 inch)
rectangular cake board

375 g (12 oz) bought chocolate-chip
cake or other flavoured loaf cake
with sloping sides

double quantity plain Buttercream
(see page 15)

1 tablespoon cocoa powder dissolved
in 1 tablespoon boiling water

green paste food colouring

icing sugar, for dusting

50 g (2 oz) each blue, red and green
ready-to-roll icing

200 g (7 oz) yellow
ready-to-roll icing

150 g (5 oz) pack chocolate sticks

200 g (7 oz) luxury milk chocolate

65 g (2½ oz) chocolate fingers

125 g (4 oz) pink ready-to-roll icing

50 g (2 oz) grey ready-to-roll icing

1 multi-pack of coloured writing
icing to include black, red, yellow
and green

50 g (2 oz) desiccated coconut

1 Put the cakes on the board. Cut the loaf cake into 3 and use buttercream to stick one piece on top of each of the other cakes for the roofs. Spoon one-third of the remaining buttercream into a bowl and flavour the remainder with cocoa paste. Spread plain buttercream all over one house, then colour any remaining icing green. Spread all the chocolate buttercream over the other houses.

2 Dust your work surface with icing sugar and roll out the blue icing. Cut out a door shape for the first house. Roll out the green and red icing and add doors and doorknobs to the other houses.

3 Make the house of straw. Knead and roll out the yellow icing. Cut it into 4 squares, each 5 x 5 cm (2 x 2 inches), mark lines with a knife to look like straw, then press them on to the cake.

4 Make the house of sticks. Cover the house with the green door with chocolate sticks, sticking some on the roof at angles.

5 Make the house of bricks. Cut the bar of chocolate into pieces and stick them over the front and sides of the last cake, adding a double square for the chimney. Add finger biscuits for the roof.

6 Shape the pigs. For each pig use 3 balls of pink ready-to-roll icing, a large ball for the body, a medium-sized ball for the head and a small ball for the nose. Add tiny balls, shaped into points, for ears and larger balls for feet, each with 3 small cuts. Roll tiny ropes and twist them into tails.

7 Make a wolf in the same way with the grey icing, but shape the circular head into more of a snout and mark the sides of the head to look like whiskers. Position the pigs and wolf on and by the houses, sticking any parts together with water. Mark nostrils with a knife and pipe on black eyes.

8 Spread green buttercream thinly over the cake board, colour the coconut green and scatter it over the board. Complete the houses with numbers piped on to the doors.

quick tip

- If you're short of time, leave the cake board undecorated and simply arrange the cakes on a green foil tray.

football boots

serves 14

decoration time 30 minutes

2 x 20 cm (8 inch) bought or homemade Swiss Rolls (see page 12)

2 tablespoons smooth apricot jam

icing sugar or cornflour, for dusting

500 g (1 lb) black ready-to-roll icing

125 g (4 oz) grey ready-to-roll icing

125 g (4 oz) white ready-to-roll icing

3 flat liquorice bootlaces

large tissue-lined shoe box

about 10 foil-wrapped chocolate footballs

1 Use a small, sharp knife to round off 2 ends of each of the Swiss rolls to make the heels. Out of the top of each cake scoop an oval, about 10 x 5 cm (4 x 2 inches) and 2 cm (¾ inch) deep in the centre. Make a sloping cut from the front of the scooped-out area down to the front end of each cake. Round off all the edges. Brush the jam over the cakes.

2 Dust your work surface with icing sugar or cornflour and roll out half the black icing to a rectangle, 30 x 20 cm (12 x 8 inches). Lay the icing over one cake, pressing it down into the cavity. Ease the icing to fit around the sides and tuck the ends under the boot. Dust the palms of your hands with icing sugar or cornflour and smooth the icing. Cover the other cake with the remaining black icing in the same way.

3 Roll out half the grey icing into 2 ovals, each 11 x 6 cm (4½ x 2½ inches), and press them into the cavities in the tops of the boots. Halve the reserved grey icing and shape 2 boot tongues, each about 12 cm (5 inches) long and 6 cm (2½ inches) across the top. Use a dampened paintbrush to secure them in position. (If the ends of the flaps flop into the cavity, prop them up with some crumpled kitchen paper until the icing has hardened.)

4 Roll out the white icing and cut it into long strips about 2 cm (¾ inch) wide. Arrange them on the boots, rounding off the corners at the front and tucking the ends around the back.

5 Cut the liquorice into 14 pieces, each about 4 cm (1½ inches) long, and use them for the laces, making holes in the white icing so that you can easily press in the ends. Use longer lengths of liquorice for the trailing ends.

6 Line a shoe box with tissue paper and arrange the boots in the box. Scatter the foil-wrapped footballs around the cakes.

quick tip

• **For quick football boots shape 2 Swiss rolls as described for the Ballet Shoes (see page 26) but cover them with black ready-to-roll icing with a paler grey liner. Add studs made with balls of black icing, coloured flashes made with strips of green or red ready-to-roll icing, and laces of liquorice or black icing.**

box of toys

serves 24

decoration time 30 minutes

18 cm (7 inch) square bought or homemade Rich Fruit Cake, covered with almond paste (see pages 11 and 21 for recipe and technique)

25 cm (10 inch) square plate or cake board

icing sugar or cornflour, for dusting

500 g (1 lb) white ready-to-roll icing

250 g (8 oz) dark green ready-to-roll icing

25 g (1 oz) red ready-to-roll icing

selection of small wooden or plastic toys for decoration

1 tube green or red writing icing

1 metre (39 inches) fine red ribbon

1 Put the cake on the plate or board. Dust your work surface with icing sugar or cornflour and roll out the white icing to a 30 cm (12 inch) square. Lay it over the cake, smoothing the icing around the sides and trimming off the excess around the base.

2 Thinly roll out the green icing to a 23 cm (9 inch) square. Use a sharp knife to trim the edges into deep scallops.

3 Lightly brush the top of the cake with a dampened paintbrush and lay the green icing over the cake so that the scalloped edges fall around the sides.

4 Roll the red icing into small balls and secure one to the tip of each scallop. Arrange the small toys on top of the cake, securing them with dots of writing icing. Tie the ribbon around the base.

quick tip

• The best place to buy little toys for decorating this cake is a toy shop with a good selection of tiny 'stocking fillers'. Add to these a few small cake decorations – Santas and snowmen – and you'll quickly accumulate a colourful collection. Remove them all from the cake before cutting.

animal ark

serves 28

decoration time about 1½ hours

3 x 375 g (12 oz) packs of fun-size flaked chocolate bars

12 cm (5 inch) and 18 cm (7 inch) square bought or homemade Rich Chocolate Cakes (see page 10)

triple quantity chocolate Buttercream (see page 15)

25 cm (10 inch) square plate

200 g (7 oz) pink ready-to-roll icing

200 g (7 oz) chocolate brown ready-to-roll icing

200 g (7 oz) light brown ready-to-roll icing

200 g (7 oz) yellow ready-to-roll icing

black food colouring

1 Trim the flaked chocolate bars so that they are 1 cm (½ inch) longer than the cakes. Cut each cake into 3 layers and then sandwich with buttercream. Put the larger cake on the plate and spread it with more buttercream. Position the smaller cake on top and spread with the remaining buttercream.

2 Using a fine-bladed knife, carefully cut each chocolate bar in half. Position the pieces around the sides of the cakes.

3 Make the elephants. For each roll out a small ball of pink icing into an oval. Press it into the buttercream. Take a larger ball of icing and mould a flattened pear shape, gradually elongating the thin end into a trunk. Cut off the tip of the trunk and impress lines along it with a knife. Prop the icing against the pink base, securing it with a dampened paintbrush. Shape and secure large floppy ears.

4 Make the monkeys. For each roll a small ball of chocolate brown icing for the head and press it into the buttercream. Shape large round ears and secure them to the sides of the head. Secure a flattened ball of light brown icing for the snout.

5 Make the lions. For each roll out a small ball of yellow icing into an oval and press it into the buttercream. Flatten a piece of brown icing for the mane and indent it around the edges with your fingertips. Roll another ball of icing and flatten it against the mane. Position it on the yellow base. Add ears and a thin rope of icing for the tail.

6 Make the bears. For each roll out a small ball of light brown icing into an oval and press it into the buttercream. Roll a larger ball of icing and position it for the head, adding 2 small, round ears. Secure a flattened ball of icing for the snout. Make paws from the icing trimmings. Use a fine paintbrush and black food colouring to add features to the animals' faces.

quick tips

- Rich and chocolaty, this cake would make a great 'alternative' christening cake.

- The animals are a bit fiddly, but you can make them several weeks in advance and store them in an airtight container, so that you can complete the cake a couple of days in advance.

princess cakes

makes 12

decoration time 20 minutes

single quantity Buttercream
(see page 15)

pink food colouring

12 bought or homemade Fairy Cakes
(see page 13)

edible silver balls

1 Divide the buttercream in half and add a few drops of pink food colouring to one bowl. Mix well to colour the buttercream. Use a small palette knife to spread the pink buttercream over the tops of the cakes to within 5 mm (¼ inch) of the edges, doming it up slightly in the centre.

2 Put half the white buttercream in a piping bag fitted with a writing nozzle and the remainder in a bag fitted with a star nozzle. Pipe lines, 1 cm (½ inch) apart, across the pink buttercream, then across in the other direction to make a diamond pattern.

3 Use the icing in the other bag to pipe little stars around the edges. Decorate the piped lines with silver balls.

quick tip

- **If you can find them, use silver-coloured paper cake cases to make these little cakes even more suitable for a princess.**

flower garden

makes 12

decoration time 30 minutes

12 bought or homemade **Fairy Cakes**
(see page 13)

single quantity green **Buttercream**
(see page 15)

icing sugar or cornflour, for dusting

375 g (12 oz) white
ready-to-roll icing

1 tube pink gel writing icing

1 If necessary, trim the tops of the cakes to level them, then spread them with green buttercream.

2 Dust your work surface with icing sugar or cornflour and knead and roll out the white icing. Stamp out flower shapes using 2.5 cm (1 inch) and 1 cm (½ inch) cutters. Curve the flowers by pressing them into a clean, dry sponge or the cupped palm of your hand with the handle of a wooden spoon. Alternatively, if you have them, use plunger cutters.

3 Arrange the flowers randomly over the cakes. Finish each flower with a dot of pink gel icing. Arrange on a plate or cake board to serve.

quick tips

• You can buy tiny cutters, often described as aspic cutters, in good cookshops or specialist cake-decorating shops, where they may be available with easy-to-press-out plungers.

• If you have lots of food to prepare for a party, cook the cakes in advance and pack them into a plastic bag or box when they are cold. Prepare the buttercream in advance and put it in a small plastic box. Freeze both until the day before the party. Decorate the cakes the night before or on the morning of the party.

funny faces

makes 12

decoration time 20 minutes

75 g (3 oz) luxury dark cooking chocolate, broken into pieces

12 bought or homemade Fairy Cakes (see page 13)

single quantity Buttercream (see page 15)

pink or brown paste food colouring

selection of small covered chocolate drops

1 tube red writing icing

sugar flowers (optional)

1 Set a heatproof bowl over a small saucepan of water. Bring the water to the boil, then remove from the heat. Add the chocolate to the bowl and leave for 2–3 minutes until melted.

2 If the cakes have high domes, trim them slightly to level them. Colour the buttercream to a skin tone, then spread it over the tops of the cakes.

3 Add sweets for eyes and pipe on red mouths. Stir the chocolate and spoon it into a greaseproof paper piping bag. Snip off the tip and pipe on hair, glasses and eye details. Add sugar flowers to the girls' hair styles if you like, then leave the cakes in a cool place until the chocolate has set.

quick tips

• You can use coloured tubes of writing icing for hair instead of the melted chocolate.

• Use the ideas here as a starting point to add a more personal touch and decorate the cakes to look like the members of your family or your child's friends. If you have time, shape ready-to-roll icing hats, scarves, bowties or even arms and legs.

• Make these cakes multiracial by colouring the buttercream with pink food colouring, melted chocolate or brown food colouring.

dominoes

makes 18

decoration time 20 minutes

30 x 23 x 5 cm (12 x 9 x 2 inch) plain or orange-flavoured Basic Sponge Cake (see page 9)

double quantity vanilla- or orange-flavoured Buttercream (see page 15)

2 tubes covered chocolate drops

50 g (2 oz) strawberry-flavoured bootlaces

1 With the longest edge of the cake nearest you, cut it into 3 bars, each 7 cm (3 inches) wide. Cut each piece into 6 small bars.

2 Spread buttercream over the top of the cakes and then decorate with groups of coloured sweets to resemble domino dots. Separate the 2 sets of dots with a strip of bootlace and then press lengths of bootlace around the edges of the cakes to make borders. Arrange on a plate or cake board and serve.

quick tips

- Plain uncut cake can be frozen and then decorated with buttercream and frozen without the sweets. Alternatively, use bought cake bars. These are ideal if you have only a couple of children for tea because they are so quick to defrost.

- You could also make the cakes into little sums by stamping out numbers, crosses for addition and multiplication, single strips for subtraction and double strips for the equals signs.

ladybirds

makes 12

decoration time 30 minutes

2 tablespoons raspberry or strawberry jam

12 bought or homemade Fairy Cakes (see page 13)

icing sugar or cornflour, for dusting

175 g (6 oz) red ready-to-roll icing

125 g (4 oz) black ready-to-roll icing

15 g (½ oz) white ready-to-roll icing

small piece of candied orange peel, cut into matchstick lengths

1 Use a pastry brush to cover the top of each cake with jam. Dust your work surface with icing sugar or cornflour and knead the red ready-to-roll icing. Roll it out thinly and cut 12 circles with a plain 6 cm (2½ inch) biscuit cutter. Put a red circle on top of each cake.

2 Roll out thin strips of black ready-to-roll icing and position one across each red circle, securing with a dampened paintbrush. Roll out half the remaining black icing to a thin sausage shape, about 1 cm (½ inch) in diameter. Cut it into thin slices and secure to the cakes to represent ladybird spots.

3 From the remaining black icing shape oval heads and secure them in position. Roll small balls of the white ready-to-roll icing for eyes and press tiny balls of black icing over them. Secure with a dampened paintbrush.

4 Make the ladybirds' antennae. Press the lengths of candied orange peel into position behind the heads, pressing small balls of black icing on the ends. Use tiny pieces of white icing to shape smiling mouths.

quick tip

• If you cannot find candied orange peel, which is cut into strips and used for the antennae, use small chocolate sticks instead.

building bricks

makes 9

decoration time 30 minutes

20 cm (8 inch) square homemade
plain or flavoured Basic Sponge Cake
(see page 9)

double quantity Buttercream
(see page 15)

500 g (1 lb) red ready-to-roll icing

icing sugar or cornflour, for dusting

500 g (1 lb) blue ready-to-roll icing

500 g (1 lb) yellow ready-to-roll
icing

2 tubes covered chocolate drops

1 tube yellow writing icing

1 tube red writing icing

candles and candle-holders (optional)

1 If necessary, level the surface of the cake and then cut it into 9 even-sized blocks.

2 Spread the tops and sides of the cake blocks thinly with buttercream, leaving the bases plain.

3 Lightly knead the red icing, then roll it out thinly on a surface lightly dusted with icing sugar or cornflour to a 38 x 20 cm (15 x 8 inch) rectangle. Cut it into 15 squares, then stick them on to the cakes. Repeat with the blue, then the yellow icing, until all the butter-iced sides of the cakes are covered.

4 Stick sweets around the edges of the cakes with writing icing, then pipe letters or numbers. Stack the cakes on a cake board, adding candles to the tops of some of the cakes, if you like.

quick tips

- Larger packs of ready-coloured ready-to-roll icing can be bought from specialist cake-decorating shops. If you don't have one near you, colour plain white icing with paste food colourings instead.

- For very little children, the blocks could be cut smaller, making 16 instead, but do allow extra time as they will be more fiddly to ice.

counting cakes

makes 12

decoration time 15 minutes

single quantity Buttercream
(see page 15)

green or yellow food colouring

12 bought or homemade Fairy Cakes
(see page 13)

icing sugar or cornflour, for dusting

175 g (6 oz) white ready-to-roll icing

50 g (2 oz) red ready-to-roll icing

50 g (2 oz) blue ready-to-roll icing

coloured sugar strands

1 Colour the buttercream with green or yellow food colouring and use a small palette knife to spread it all over the tops of the cakes.

2 Dust your work surface with icing sugar or cornflour. Knead the white ready-to-roll icing, roll it out and use a plain 6 cm (2½ inch) round biscuit cutter to cut out 12 circles. Gently press one on the top of each cake.

3 Roll out the red ready-to-roll icing and cut out half the numbers. Secure to the cakes with a dampened paintbrush. Use the blue ready-to-roll icing for the remaining numbers.

4 Lightly brush the edges of the white icing with a dampened paintbrush and scatter over the sugar strands.

quick tip

• Cut out the numbers by hand using a sharp knife or use small number biscuit cutters. The numbers could simply run from 1 to 12, or you could represent the ages of the party-goers, if appropriate.

chocolate hedgehogs

makes 6

decoration time 20 minutes

6 bought or homemade Fairy Cakes (see page 13)

single quantity dark Chocolate Fudge Icing (see page 18)

3 flaked chocolate bars, cut into thin pieces

3 glacé cherries, halved

12 edible silver balls or small covered chocolate drops

1 Remove the cakes from the paper cases and cut a triangular snout in each cake. Put them on a wire rack set over a large plate.

2 Spoon warm chocolate icing over the cakes until they are completely covered. Working quickly, stick pieces of flaked chocolate over two-thirds of each cake to represent the spines. Add cherry noses and silver-ball or chocolate-drop eyes.

3 Carefully lift the hedgehogs on to a cake board or plate, trimming away any surplus icing around the base.

quick tips

• If children are helping you make the cakes, it might be easier to ice and decorate them one at a time, because the icing sets quickly, making it more difficult to press the chocolate spines on to the cakes.

• Nestle the hedgehogs on a grassy board by colouring a little desiccated coconut with liquid green food colouring and spooning it around the finished cakes.

space bugs

makes 12

decoration time 25 minutes

12 chocolate or plain, bought or homemade Fairy Cakes (see page 13)

4 tablespoons chocolate spread

icing sugar or cornflour, for dusting

375 g (12 oz) red ready-to-roll icing

12 chocolate-covered marshmallows

12 chocolate sticks

1 tube red writing icing

1 pack small covered chocolate drops

1 tube black writing icing

1 Leave the cakes in their paper cases and, if necessary, trim the tops to level them. Spread the cakes with chocolate spread.

2 Dust your work surface with icing sugar or cornflour. Knead the red ready-to-roll icing, roll it out and cut 12 rounds with a plain 5.5 cm (2¼ inch) biscuit cutter. Cut a little off the top of each round using the same cutter, then cut the remaining shapes in half to make wings. Press the wings on to the cakes so that the tips are slightly apart. Re-roll the trimmings as needed and continue until all the cakes are covered.

3 Add the marshmallows for heads, sticking them in place with a little extra chocolate spread if necessary. Halve the chocolate sticks and press 2 behind each head for antennae. Pipe on red smiling mouths, pipe dots of red icing over the wings and stick on the sweets. Add chocolate-drop eyes to the faces and the tops of the antennae in the same way. Pipe black icing dots on the eyes. Arrange the bugs on a cake board or plate. Leave in a cool place to harden.

quick tips

- If you don't have a biscuit cutter the right size, use an upturned glass as a template.

- Look out for ready-coloured icing from specialist cake-decorating shops. Supermarkets do sell coloured icing, but it is usually in a box containing 3 or 4 small packs of different colours and can be expensive if you only need one. Alternatively, buy white icing and colour it yourself with red paste colouring.

- For Halloween make up death-watch beetles with brown or black ready-to-roll icing. Omit the spots or pipe on squiggly markings with tubes of coloured writing icing.

on the farm

makes 12

decoration time 45 minutes

½ **quantity Buttercream**
(see page 15)

12 bought or homemade Fairy Cakes
(see pages 13)

100 g (3½ oz) brown
ready-to-roll icing

icing sugar or cornflour, for dusting

100 g (3½ oz) yellow
ready-to-roll icing

100 g (3½ oz) pink
ready-to-roll icing

15 g (½ oz) white ready-to-roll icing

15 g (½ oz) black ready-to-roll icing

black food colouring

1 Use a palette knife to spread a thick layer of the buttercream over 4 of the cakes and lightly peak (these will become the sheep). Spread the rest of the buttercream over the remaining cakes.

2 Make the sheep. Take 75 g (3 oz) of the brown ready-to-roll icing, wrapping the remainder in clingfilm. Dust your work surface with icing sugar or cornflour and knead the icing. Reserve a small piece for the ears and roll the remainder into 4 balls. Flatten each ball into an oval shape and gently press on the cakes thickly spread with buttercream. Shape and position small ears on each sheep.

3 Make the cows. Reserve a small piece of the yellow ready-to-roll icing for the ears. Roll the remainder into 4 balls and flatten into ovals as large as the cake tops. Gently press on to 4 more cakes. Shape and position the ears. Use the remaining brown ready-to-roll icing to shape the cows' nostrils and horns, securing with a dampened paintbrush.

4 Make the pigs. Reserve 25 g (1 oz) of the pink ready-to-roll icing for the snouts and ears. Roll the remainder into 4 balls and flatten them into rounds, almost as large as each cake top. Shape and position the snouts and floppy ears, pressing 2 small holes in each snout with the tip of a cocktail stick or fine skewer.

5 Use the white and black icing to make all the animals' eyes, changing the shape and size to suit each animal. Roll small balls of white icing and press tiny balls of black icing over them. Secure with a dampened paintbrush. Use a fine paintbrush, dipped in the black food colouring, to paint on additional features.

quick tip

- Lightly dusting your work surface with icing sugar or cornflour will help stop the icing sticking to the surface and will smooth and polish the icing when it's on the cake. Cornflour is better if you're working with dark reds and blues because it disappears as you smooth, while icing sugar may leave a faint white mark.

snakes in the jungle

makes 12

decoration time 45 minutes

2 tablespoons strawberry or raspberry jam

12 bought or homemade Fairy Cakes (see page 13)

icing sugar or cornflour, for dusting

175 g (6 oz) green ready-to-roll icing

4 flaked chocolate bars, cut into 5 cm (2 inch) lengths

50 g (2 oz) red ready-to-roll icing

50 g (2 oz) yellow ready-to-roll icing

50 g (2 oz) white ready-to-roll icing

25 g (1 oz) black ready-to-roll icing

1 Use a pastry brush to cover the top of each cake with jam. Dust your work surface with icing sugar or cornflour and knead the green ready-to-roll icing. Roll it out thinly and cut 12 circles with a plain 6 cm (2½ inch) biscuit cutter. Put a green circle on top of each cake.

2 Make a snake. Take about 7 g (¼ oz) of ready-to-roll icing and roll it under the palm of your hand to form a thin sausage about 12–15 cm (5–6 inches) long, tapering it to a point at one end and shaping a head at the other. Flatten the head slightly and mark a mouth with a small, sharp knife.

3 Thinly roll out a little ready-to-roll icing in a contrasting colour and cut out small diamond shapes. Secure along the snake using a dampened paintbrush. Wrap the snake around a length of flaked chocolate and position on top of a cake.

4 Make more snakes in the same way, kneading together small amounts of the coloured ready-to-roll icing to make different colours. For some of the cakes, press the chocolate bar vertically into the cake.

5 To make the snakes' eyes roll small balls of white icing and press tiny balls of black icing over them. Secure to the snakes' heads with a dampened paintbrush.

quick tip

- As long as you have green icing for the cake bases you can make the snakes in any colours you like. Orange can easily be made by blending red and yellow icing, and pink by blending red and white.

2
birthday cakes

big birthday

serves 45–50

decoration time 1 hour

15 cm (6 inch), 20 cm (8 inch) and 25 cm (10 inch) round bought or homemade Basic Sponge Cakes (see page 9) or Rich Chocolate Cakes (see page 10)

30 cm (12 inch) plate

quadruple quantity Buttercream (see page 15) or triple quantity White Chocolate Ganache (see page 17)

icing sugar or cornflour, for dusting

200 g (7 oz) dark red ready-to-roll icing

200 g (7 oz) dark blue ready-to-roll icing

200 g (7 oz) purple ready-to-roll icing

1 tube red or blue writing icing

number birthday candles (e.g., 18 or 21)

fine blue and purple parcel ribbon

1 Put the largest cake on the plate and spread it with a scant half of the buttercream or ganache, smoothing it with a palette knife.

2 Put the medium-sized cake on top and spread it with more buttercream or ganache in the same way. Position the smallest cake on top and spread it evenly with the remaining buttercream or ganache.

3 Dust your work surface with icing sugar or cornflour and shape the coloured icings into little parcel shapes. Use the writing icing to pipe ribbons on the parcels.

4 Position the candles on top of the cake, then drape lengths of ribbon over the top and down the sides of the cake. Tuck the parcels in among the ribbons.

quick tips

- Celebratory candles are available in all numbers, so this is a quick and easy celebration cake for any important birthday.

- Cover the cake with buttercream or ganache a day in advance and keep it in a cool place.

- The cake can also be decorated with ready-to-roll icing. You will need about 2 kg (4 lb). Cover each cake separately with icing before stacking them on the plate.

50th birthday

serves 30

preparation time 10 minutes,
plus cooling

cooking time about
50 minutes

decoration time 1 hour

large 5 and 0 number cake tins

**2 x 5-egg quantity Basic Sponge
Cake mixture (see page 9)**

**double quantity Buttercream
(see page 15)**

**8 tablespoons smooth raspberry or
strawberry jam**

icing sugar or cornflour, for dusting

**750 g (1½ lb) pale blue
ready-to-roll icing**

**45 x 35 cm (18 x 14 inches)
rectangular cake board**

**300 g (10 oz) chocolate brown
ready-to-roll icing**

**1 kg (2 lb) dark blue
ready-to-roll icing**

8–10 tea lights

**2 metres (6 feet) brown ribbon for
edges of cake board**

1 Grease and line the number tins and put them on a large baking sheet. Divide the cake mixture between the tins and level the surface. Bake in a preheated oven, 160°C (325°F), Gas Mark 3, for about 50 minutes or until just firm and a skewer, inserted into the centres, comes out clean. Leave to cool.

2 Cut the cakes in half horizontally and sandwich the layers with the buttercream and half the jam. Spread the remaining jam over the tops and sides of the cakes.

3 Dust your work surface with icing sugar or cornflour and roll out 500 g (1 lb) of the pale blue icing to a rectangle that is slightly smaller than the cake board. Dampen the board and lift the icing on to the board. Smooth it down gently with the palms of your hands and trim the icing, leaving a border 2 cm (¾ inch) wide around the edges of the board.

4 Thinly roll out 200 g (7 oz) of the brown icing and cut out long strips. Use these to cover the edges of the board, trimming off the excess around the edges. Reserve the trimmings.

5 Roll out half the dark blue icing and use it to cover one of the numbers, easing the icing down the sides and trimming off the excess around the base. If necessary patch up any gaps around the sides. Carefully transfer the cake to the board. Cover the second cake with the remaining icing and put it on the board.

6 Roll the remaining pale blue and brown icing into long, thin ropes. Twist them together and cut into manageable lengths. Drape over the cakes, securing with a dampened paintbrush. Arrange the tea lights around the numbers and secure the brown ribbon around the sides of the board.

quick tips

- **This is a great cake for a large party of adults. It cuts into plenty of portions, is not too difficult to ice and works well for any age. Large number tins can be hired for a couple of days for making the cake.**

- **It's easier to ice the centres of numbers such as 0, 6, 8 and 9 with a strip of icing before you cover the rest of the cake.**

birthday present

serves 40

decoration time 30 minutes

23 cm (9 inch) square bought or homemade Rich Fruit Cake, covered with almond paste (see pages 11 and 21 for recipe and technique)

30 cm (12 inch) square cake board

1.5 kg (3 lb) white ready-to-roll icing

dark red or pink food colouring

icing sugar or cornflour, for dusting

2 metres (6 feet) soft grey ribbon, about 2.5 cm (1 inch) wide

2 metres (6 feet) pale pink ribbon, about 5 cm (2 inches) wide

pale pink ribbon for edges of cake board

1 Put the cake on the board. Reserve 200 g (7 oz) of the icing and lightly knead the remainder. Use a cocktail stick to dot the icing carefully and cautiously with food colouring. The more colour you add, the more vibrant the finished result will be.

2 Roll out the icing to a thick sausage. Fold it into 3 and roll again, repeating the process until the icing is marbled with colour. Dust your work surface with icing sugar or cornflour and roll out the icing to a square that will cover the cake. Smooth the icing down the sides and trim off the excess around the base.

3 Lay the narrower ribbon over the wider ribbon. Use the tip of a knife to tuck the ends of the ribbons under the base of the cake on one side. Bring the ribbons over to the other side and cut to fit, tucking the ends under the cake. Repeat on the other 2 sides and shape a generous bow for the top. Secure the bow in position with clear adhesive tape.

4 Use the reserved white icing to cover the edges of the cake board. Secure the pink ribbon around the edges of the board.

quick tips

- The ribbons are the focal point of this easy cake, so choose soft, delicate colours for a romantic look, or use an alternative colour scheme for a bolder effect.

- Instead of fruit cake, you could use a bought or homemade sponge cake, sandwiched with buttercream.

man's best friend

serves 24

decoration time about 1 hour

25 cm (10 inch) round bought or homemade Basic Sponge Cake (see page 9) or Rich Chocolate Cake (see page 10)

triple quantity Chocolate Fudge Icing (see page 18)

30 cm (12 inch) round plate

425 g (14 oz) light brown ready-to-roll icing

icing sugar or cornflour, for dusting

200 g (7 oz) blue ready-to-roll icing

dark blue or black food colouring

1 Halve the cake horizontally and sandwich the layers together with one-third of the chocolate fudge icing. Put it on the plate and use a palette knife to swirl the remainder of the fudge icing over the top and sides of the cake.

2 Make the dog. Roll a 200 g (7 oz) ball of brown icing for the body and flatten it slightly. Put it on the centre of the cake. Roll a 175 g (6 oz) ball of icing for the head. Pinch one side to a point to make a muzzle. Rest the head, tilting it slightly to one side, at one end of the body. From the remaining icing shape small paws, droopy ears and a curved tail. Position the paws and ears and reserve the tail.

3 Dust your work surface with icing sugar or cornflour and thinly roll out the blue icing. Cut out a 20 cm (8 inch) square. Drape the icing over the cake, fitting it first around the dog's head and draping it across the cake in loose folds. Position the tail.

4 Use a fine paintbrush and the blue or black food colouring to paint closed eyes, a nose and a mouth on the dog's face.

quick tip

• It's not only children who like animal cakes – there are plenty of adults who would find this cake appealing. The dog can easily be made to resemble the recipient's own dog by changing the colour of the icing and by painting on spots or patches as appropriate.

triple chocolate croquembouche

serves 10–12

preparation time 20 minutes

cooking time 20 minutes

decoration time 30 minutes

40 Choux Pastry Buns (see page 14)

double quantity White Chocolate Ganache (see page 17)

200 g (7 oz) plain chocolate

flat plate, at least 28 cm (11 inches) across

200 g (7 oz) milk chocolate

12–15 gold-coloured chocolate dragées, roughly chopped

1 When the choux pastry buns are cool, fill each one with a heaped teaspoon of the white chocolate ganache.

2 Break half the plain chocolate into pieces and put them in a bowl over a saucepan of lightly simmering water until the chocolate has melted. Dip the base of about 10 buns in the melted chocolate and arrange them in a circle, about 23 cm (9 inches) across, on the serving plate. (When it sets, the chocolate will hold the buns together.) Put about 3 buns in the centre.

3 Gradually build up layers of buns to form a cone shape, dipping each bun in melted chocolate so that it is secured to the buns underneath. Finish with a single bun on top.

4 Melt the remaining plain chocolate and the milk chocolate in separate bowls and spoon over the buns. Tuck the chocolate dragées in among the buns to finish. Keep the cake in a cool place until ready to serve.

quick tips

- Make the buns in advance, put them in plastic bags and freeze them, crisping them in a moderate oven for 5 minutes before use.

- If you're assembling the croquembouche in hot weather you might need to chill it halfway through so that it doesn't collapse.

white chocolate frosted cake

serves 12

decoration time 20 minutes

18 cm (7 inch) round bought or homemade Basic Sponge Cake (see page 9)

single quantity White Chocolate Ganache (see page 17)

25 cm (10 inch) round or square cream-coloured plate

8–10 large, cream-coloured, silk flowers

1 Cut the cake in half horizontally, sandwich the layers together with a little of the ganache and put the cake on the plate.

2 Use a palette knife to spread the remaining ganache over the top and sides of the cake. Finish by swirling it in vertical strokes around the sides.

3 Cut the stems of the flowers down to about 5 cm (2 inches). Alternatively, twist the stems under each flower so they can be reshaped and used again. Arrange the flowers over the top of the cake.

quick tips

- The flavours of this simple cake are good enough to enjoy just as they are. However, if you want some extra zing, try using a spicy or an orange- or lemon-flavoured sponge base or drizzle the cake with a coffee- or citrus-flavoured liqueur before sandwiching the layers together.

- You can use delicate silk flowers to decorate the cake or more flamboyant ones – it's a matter of personal preference.

box of chocolates

serves 18

decoration time 30 minutes

18 cm (7 inch) square bought or homemade Rich Chocolate Cake (see page 10)

23 cm (9 inch) square flat plate

single quantity Dark Chocolate Ganache (see page 17)

4 x 100 g (3½ oz) chocolate bars, each 19 x 9 cm (7½ x 3½ inches)

500 g (1 lb) selection of chocolates

150 g (5 oz) chocolate truffles

1.5 metres (5 feet) chocolate-coloured ribbon, about 4 cm (1½ inches) wide

1 Put the cake on the plate and spread the ganache over the top and sides, smoothing it into an even layer with a palette knife.

2 Unwrap the chocolate bars and gently press a bar against each side of the cake so they meet squarely at the corners.

3 Arrange the chocolates and truffles over the top of the cake so that they resemble a layer in a box of chocolates. Wrap the ribbon around the sides of the cake, tying it in a bow.

quick tip

• Use plain or milk chocolate bars for the sides of the cake but choose thin bars rather than chunky ones. Remove them before you cut the cake into portions.

chocobloc

serves 8–10

decoration time 30 minutes

15 cm (6 inch) square bought or
homemade Rich Chocolate Cake
(see page 10)

single quantity Dark Chocolate
Ganache (see page 17)

35 x 28 cm (14 x 11 inches)
rectangular marble slab or
cake board

4 tablespoons apricot jam

plenty of gold foil (e.g., chocolate
bar wrappings)

icing sugar or cornflour, for dusting

250 g (8 oz) purple
ready-to-roll icing

1 Slice any dome off the top of the cake. Cut a slice 8 cm (3¼ inches) wide off the cake and then cut off (and discard) one-third of the slice to leave 2 rectangular pieces. Halve each horizontally and sandwich them with ganache. Put the larger cake on the marble slab or board and brush both cakes with apricot jam.

2 While the ganache is still fairly runny, spoon a little over both cake pieces, spreading it down the sides so they are completely covered. Leave for about 10 minutes to firm up a little, then cover with the remaining ganache.

3 Transfer the chocolate bar to the marble or board and cut off a few pieces. Score the markings in the chocolate bar with a sharp knife.

4 Wrap one end of the chocolate cake in a strip of the gold foil. Dust your work surface with icing sugar or cornflour and roll out the purple icing to a rectangle, 22 x 14 cm (8¾ x 5½ inches). Lay it over the cake so that one edge rests over the foil strip. Tear more foil into jagged pieces and tuck under the other end of the icing.

5 Shape the icing trimmings and a little more gold foil into 'torn' wrappings and scatter them around the cake.

quick tip

- First, cover the parts of the cake that won't be hidden under icing or foil with the ganache, before it starts to thicken. Slide a piece of greaseproof paper under the wire rack to catch the ganache that falls through – you can scrape it up and spread it over areas of the cake that won't be visible.

chocolate truffle cake

serves 18

decoration time 30 minutes

3 x 140 g (4½ oz) packs chocolate sticks

20 cm (8 inch) round bought or homemade Rich Chocolate Cake (see page 10)

25–28 cm (10–11 inch) round plate

single quantity Dark Chocolate Ganache or double quantity Chocolate Fudge Icing (see page 17 or 18)

300 g (10 oz) bought or homemade chocolate truffles

50 g (2 oz) pink crystallized roses

1.5 metres (5 feet) pink ribbon, 4–5 cm (1½–2 inches) wide

1 Trim the chocolate sticks so that they are 1 cm (½ inch) taller than the depth of the cake. Put the cake on the plate and use a palette knife to spread the ganache or fudge icing over the top and sides.

2 While the icing is still soft, secure the chocolate sticks, spacing them fractionally apart, around the sides of the cake.

3 Arrange the truffles over the top of the cake and scatter over the roses. Tie the ribbon around the cake, finishing with a bow.

quick tip

• If you prefer to make your own chocolate truffles, heat 125 ml (4 fl oz) double cream in a small pan until it bubbles around the edges. Remove it from the heat and stir in 250 g (8 oz) chopped plain chocolate. Leave until the chocolate has melted, then turn the mixture into a bowl and flavour it with 2 tablespoons orange or coffee liqueur, brandy or rum. Chill until firm enough to roll into small balls and dust with cocoa powder.

confetti meringue

serves 8–10

preparation time 15 minutes

cooking time about 1¼ hours

decoration time 20 minutes

4 egg whites

225 g (7½ oz) caster sugar

300 ml (½ pint) double cream

1 tablespoon icing sugar

1–2 tablespoons rosewater

flat round glass plate, about 25 cm (10 inches) in diameter

6–8 small pink roses

2 tablespoons bought or homemade pink sugar crystals

1 Line 2 baking sheets with nonstick baking paper. To make the meringue, whisk the egg whites in a thoroughly clean bowl until stiff. Add the sugar, a tablespoon at a time, whisking well after each addition until the meringue is stiff and glossy.

2 Spread a thin 20 cm (8 inch) circle of meringue on one baking sheet for the base of the cake. Use 2 dessertspoons to place spoonfuls of meringue on the baking sheets, spacing them about 3 cm (1¼ inches) apart. (Makes about 28 meringues.) Bake in a preheated oven, 120°C (250°F), Gas Mark ½, for about 1¼ hours until the meringues are crisp, swapping the baking sheets round halfway through cooking. Leave the meringues to cool.

3 Mix the cream with the icing sugar and enough rosewater to taste, whipping them together until the mixture only just holds its shape.

4 Put the meringue circle on the serving plate. Spoon over a little of the cream, then add a circle of meringues around the edge, with 2–3 in the centre. Repeat the layering, building up the meringues into a cone and finishing with a single meringue on top.

5 Pull the petals from half the roses and scatter them over the cake. Tuck the whole roses around the base of the meringues. Just before serving, dust generously with the pink sugar.

quick tip

• To make the pink sugar, put a little caster sugar in a small bowl and add a dot of pink food colouring paste. Work the paste into the sugar with the back of a teaspoon.

frosted fruit meringue cake

serves 18

decoration time 45 minutes

3 egg whites

200 g (7 oz) caster sugar

1 fig

several small plums and apricots

10–12 cherries

75 g (3 oz) blueberries

20 cm (8 inch) round bought or homemade Basic Sponge Cake (see page 9)

single quantity Buttercream (see page 15)

6 tablespoons raspberry or strawberry jam

25 cm (10 inch) round glass plate

pinch of salt

1 Lightly whisk one egg white in a small bowl until it is broken up. Put half the caster sugar in another bowl. Using your fingers or a large paintbrush, coat the fig with egg white, then sprinkle it generously with sugar until it is evenly coated. Transfer it to a sheet of nonstick baking paper. Frost all the remaining fruits and leave them in a cool place for at least 1 hour to dry.

2 Cut the cake horizontally into three and sandwich the layers together with the buttercream and jam. Put the cake on a baking sheet.

3 Whisk the 2 remaining egg whites with the salt in a thoroughly clean bowl until stiff. Gradually whisk in the remaining caster sugar, a tablespoon at a time, whisking well after each addition until the mixture is smooth and glossy. Use a palette knife to spread a thin layer of the meringue over the top and sides of the cake to seal in any crumbs. Turn the remaining meringue on to the top of the cake and spread it over the cake evenly. Use the tip of the palette knife to mark deep swirls in the meringue.

4 Bake the cake in a preheated oven, 190°C (375°F), Gas Mark 5, for 5–10 minutes until the meringue is toasted. Rotate the baking sheet once or twice during cooking to give an even colour and take care that the meringue doesn't become too brown.

5 Remove the cake from the oven, transfer to the plate and leave to cool for a few minutes. Arrange the larger fruits on top of the cake, halving some of them if you like. Scatter the cherries and blueberries over the top.

quick tips

- The meringue must be made and cooked on the day you serve the cake, but you can bake the cake beforehand, sandwiching it and frosting the fruits a day in advance.

- For a special occasion, drizzle the sponge with lemon or orange liqueur before spreading it with buttercream.

vase of flowers

serves 12

preparation time 15 minutes, plus cooling

cooking time about 45 minutes

decoration time 20 minutes

4-egg quantity Basic Sponge Cake mixture (see page 9)

double quantity Buttercream (see page 15)

square plate

icing sugar or cornflour, for dusting

750 g (1½ lb) dark red ready-to-roll icing

small bunch of dried roses

plenty of raffia

1 Turn the cake mixture into a greased and lined cake tin, 20 cm (8 inches) square, and level the surface. Bake in a preheated oven, 160°C (325°F), Gas Mark 3, for about 45 minutes or until just firm, and a skewer, inserted in the centre, comes out clean. Leave to cool.

2 Slice the domed surface off the top of the cake and cut it into 4 equal pieces. Use half the buttercream to stack the cakes together. Transfer the cake to the plate and spread the remaining buttercream over the top and sides with a palette knife.

3 Dust your work surface with icing sugar or cornflour and roll out the red icing. Cut out 4 rectangles, each 1 cm (½ inch) longer than the depth of the cake and 11 cm (4½ inches) wide. Position a rectangle against each side of the cake, dampening the edges with a paintbrush so they stick together.

4 Cut the rose stems to 5 cm (2 inches) long and wrap the ends in clingfilm or foil. Press them into the top of the cake. Leave the icing to harden for a couple of hours or overnight, then wrap the raffia loosely around the sides.

quick tip

• Serving a tall cake like this can be awkward. It will be easier if you remove the raffia and flowers first and then split the cake in half horizontally so that you can serve the halves cut into squares.

feathered hat

serves 12

decoration time 30 minutes

2 x 15 cm (6 inch) round bought or
homemade Basic Sponge Cakes
(see page 9)

single quantity Buttercream
(see page 15)

6 tablespoons smooth raspberry or
strawberry jam

28 cm (11 inch) round cake board

icing sugar or cornflour, for dusting

1 kg (2 lb) ivory-coloured
ready-to-roll icing

50 cm (20 inches) bottle green wired
ribbon, about 7 cm (3 inches) wide

spray of dark green feathers

large ivory-coloured silk flower

ivory-coloured ribbon for edge of
cake board

1 Cut a slice off the top of each cake so they are about 5 cm (2 inches) deep. Cut each cake in half horizontally and sandwich the 4 layers together with half the buttercream and all the jam. Position the cake to one side of the cake board and spread the remaining buttercream over the top and sides.

2 Dust your work surface with icing sugar or cornflour and roll out 750 g (1½ lb) of the ivory-coloured icing to a circle, 28 cm (11 inches) across. Lift it over the cake and smooth the icing down the sides, trimming off any excess around the base.

3 Dampen the board with a little water. Combine the trimmings with the remaining icing and use it to cover the cake board. The easiest way to do this is to roll out the icing into a thick, curved crescent shape, roughly the same size as the exposed board area. Trim the inner curve of the crescent and lift the icing around the cake, smoothing it out to fit the board and trimming off the excess around the edges.

4 Make a loop in the centre of the green ribbon and tuck it to one side of the cake, bending the wired ends of the ribbon over the cake. Secure it to the iced board with clear adhesive tape. Position the feathers and silk flower against the side of the cake, pressing them gently into the icing. Secure the ivory-coloured ribbon around the edge of the cake board.

quick tip

- This makes a great birthday cake for a friend who's crazy about hats. Use any colour theme for the icing and decorations, which can be as traditional or as flamboyant as you like.

green fingers

serves 20

decoration time 30 minutes, plus drying

50 g (2 oz) purple ready-to-roll icing

2 cocktail sticks

50 g (2 oz) grey ready-to-roll icing

23 cm (9 inch) round bought or homemade Basic Sponge Cake (see page 9)

single quantity Buttercream (see page 15)

6 tablespoons smooth raspberry or strawberry jam

30–35 cm (12–14 inch) round wooden board

small terracotta pot, about 6 cm (2½ inches) in diameter

100 g (3½ oz) plain chocolate, finely grated

icing sugar or cornflour, for dusting

1 kg (2 lb) green ready-to-roll icing

1 small sprig of bay leaves

plenty of small sprigs of lavender leaves and flowers

1 Make the trowel by rolling the purple icing into a thick sausage. Flatten the ends and use the back of a small knife to indent markings at each end. Press 2 cocktail sticks, slightly apart, into one end. Flatten the grey icing into a scoop shape with one straight edge. Press the cocktail sticks into the straight edge and rest the trowel over a foil-covered rolling pin to harden for about 24 hours.

2 Cut the cake in half horizontally and sandwich the layers with all but 1 tablespoon of the buttercream and half the jam. Put it on the board. Use a dessertspoon to scoop out a little of the centre of the cake and pack it into the pot. Spread it with the reserved buttercream and sprinkle with a little of the grated chocolate. Scoop out a little more of the cake to make a wider cavity. Spread the remaining jam over the top and sides of the cake.

3 Dust your work surface with icing sugar or cornflour and roll out the green icing to a circle, 35 cm (14 inches) across. Lay it over the cake, easing it into the cavity and around the sides and letting the excess icing rest on the board.

4 Press the bay and a few lavender sprigs into the cake in the pot. Arrange more sprigs around the sides of the cake, securing them in the icing on the board.

5 Scatter a pile of grated chocolate over the top of the cake and in piles around the sides. Position the pot and trowel on top of the cake.

quick tip

• Herbs and herb flowers make pretty decorations and won't wilt as quickly as other fresh flowers, so if you use them you can assemble the cake a day in advance. Alternatively, use other small flowers, such as rose buds, primroses or geraniums, and position them at the last minute.

golfer's bag

serves 16

decoration time 30 minutes, plus drying

375 g (12 oz) white ready-to-roll icing

5 x 15 cm (6 inch) lengths wood or plastic dowelling

15 g (½ oz) red ready-to-roll icing

icing sugar or cornflour, for dusting

150 g (5 oz) green ready-to-roll icing

23 cm (9 inch) round cake board

2 x 15 cm (6 inch) round bought or homemade Basic Sponge Cakes (see page 9)

single quantity Buttercream (see page 15)

3 tablespoons smooth apricot jam

1 kg (2 lb) brown ready-to-roll icing

1 tube black writing icing

silver food colouring

red ribbon for edge of cake board

1 Roll 5 balls, each 25 g (1 oz), of white icing and gently indent each with the end of a paintbrush to make golf balls. Shape the heads of 5 clubs, each 40 g (1½ oz), in white icing, adding markings with a knife. Dampen the tips of the dowelling rods and press them into the ends. Shape several small tees in red icing. Leave them with the clubs and golf balls on a sheet of nonstick baking paper to dry overnight.

2 Dust your work surface with icing sugar or cornflour and roll out the green icing. Use it to cover the cake board, trimming off the excess.

3 Cut the cakes in half horizontally and sandwich them together with the buttercream. Put the stacked cakes on the board and spread the jam over the top and sides.

4 Reserve 100 g (3½ oz) of the brown icing. Roll out a further 100 g (3½ oz) of the brown icing to a circle, 15 cm (6 inches) diameter, and lay it over the top cake. Roll out the remainder and cut out a rectangle, 50 x 16 cm (20 x 6½ inches). Dampen the short edges and wrap it around the cake so that the top edge is about 2 cm (¾ inch) higher than the cakes. Smooth the join together.

5 Roll out the reserved brown icing and cut out a rectangle, 12 x 10 cm (5 x 4 inches). Dampen the edges and secure it to the bag for a pocket. Cut out a strip, 15 x 2 cm (6 x ¾ inch), and secure the ends to the bag for a handle.

6 Use the writing icing to pipe stitches over the bag. Arrange the golf balls and tees beside it.

7 Paint the clubs and rods with silver food colouring and leave to dry. Press them gently into the top of the cake and paint the backs. Secure the ribbon around the edge of the board.

quick tip

- Wood or plastic dowelling rods are available from cake-decorating shops and from DIY stores. If you buy long sticks, cut them to size before using.

triple chocolate fairy cakes

makes 12

decoration time 20 minutes

100 g (3½ oz) white chocolate, chopped

100 g (3½ oz) milk chocolate, chopped

100 g (3½ oz) plain chocolate, chopped

40 g (1½ oz) unsalted butter

12 bought or homemade chocolate Fairy Cakes (see page 13)

cocoa powder, for dusting

1 Put the white, milk and plain chocolate in separate bowls and add 15 g (½ oz) butter to each. Melt all the chocolate, either one at a time in the microwave or by resting each bowl over a saucepan of gently simmering water. Stir occasionally until melted and smooth.

2 Use a small palette knife to spread the melted white chocolate over 4 of the cakes and sprinkle with a little cocoa powder.

3 Put 2 tablespoons of the melted milk and plain chocolate in separate piping bags fitted with writing nozzles. Spread the milk chocolate over 4 more of the cakes and pipe dots of plain chocolate over the milk chocolate.

4 Spread the plain chocolate over the 4 remaining cakes and scribble with lines of piped milk chocolate.

quick tip

• When you melt chocolate in a bowl over hot water, break the chocolate into small pieces and put it in an ovenproof bowl that will stand above the water. Take care that steam from the water doesn't condense in the bowl – even a few drops of water will spoil the chocolate.

chocolate toffee fairy cakes

makes 12

cooking time 5 minutes

decoration time 15 minutes

200 g (7 oz) (about ½ can) sweetened condensed milk

50 g (2 oz) caster sugar

65 g (2½ oz) unsalted butter

2 tablespoons golden syrup

12 bought or homemade Fairy Cakes (see page 13)

100 g (3½ oz) plain chocolate, chopped

100 g (3½ oz) milk chocolate, chopped

1 Put the condensed milk, sugar, butter and golden syrup in a medium heavy-based saucepan and heat gently, stirring, until the sugar dissolves. Cook over a gentle heat, stirring, for about 5 minutes until the mixture has turned a pale fudge colour.

2 Leave the toffee to cool for 2 minutes then spoon the toffee over the top of the cakes.

3 Melt the plain and milk chocolate in separate heatproof bowls, either one at a time in the microwave or by resting each bowl over a saucepan of gently simmering water. Put a couple of teaspoons of each type of melted chocolate on to a cake, mixing up the colours, and tap the cake on the work surface to level the chocolate. Use the tip of a cocktail stick or fine skewer to swirl the chocolates together to marble them slightly. Repeat on the remaining cakes.

quick tip

- For a really quick teatime treat, use the caramel and chocolate topping on a plain bought sponge cake.

florentine fairy cakes

makes 12

cooking time 8 minutes

decoration time 10 minutes

75 g (3 oz) flaked almonds

50 g (2 oz) sultanas

125 g (4 oz) glacé cherries, quartered

4 tablespoons golden syrup

12 bought or homemade Fairy Cakes (see page 13)

50 g (2 oz) plain chocolate, broken into pieces

1 Mix together the flaked almonds, sultanas, glacé cherries and golden syrup in a bowl. Tip the mixture on to a greased baking sheet and spread in a thin layer. Bake in a preheated oven, 200°C (400°F), Gas Mark 6, for 8 minutes or until the nuts and syrup are turning golden. Remove from the oven and leave to cool slightly.

2 Break up the mixture and scatter it over the cakes in an even layer.

3 Melt the chocolate in a heatproof bowl, either in the microwave or by resting the bowl over a saucepan of gently simmering water. Put the melted chocolate in a piping bag fitted with a writing nozzle. Scribble lines of chocolate across the fruit and nut topping. Leave to set.

quick tips

• Instead of flaked almonds use a mixture of chopped nuts, if you prefer, or walnuts and almonds, finely chopped.

• Replace 25 g (1 oz) of the glacé cherries with chopped candied peel.

white chocolate curl cakes

makes 12

decoration time 15 minutes

100 g (3½ oz) chunky piece white chocolate

single quantity white Chocolate Fudge Icing (see page 18)

12 bought or homemade white chocolate chip Fairy Cakes (see page 13)

icing sugar, for dusting

1 Use a vegetable peeler to pare curls from the chocolate bar. If the chocolate breaks off in small, brittle shards, try softening it in the microwave for a few seconds first, but take care not to overheat and melt it. Set the curls aside in a cool place while you ice the cakes.

2 Use a small palette knife to spread the fudge icing all over the tops of the cakes.

3 Pile the chocolate curls on to the cakes and dust them with icing sugar.

quick tip

- Make chocolate flakes instead of curls by using the coarsest side of a grater.

strawberry creams

makes 12

decoration time 20 minutes

12 bought or homemade Fairy Cakes
(see page 13)

300 g (10 oz) small strawberries

150 ml (¼ pint) double cream

2 teaspoons caster sugar

½ teaspoon vanilla extract

4 tablespoons redcurrant jelly

1 tablespoon water

1 Use a small sharp knife to scoop out the centre of each cake to leave a deep cavity. Reserve 6 of the smallest strawberries and thinly slice the remainder.

2 Use a hand-held electric whisk to whip the cream with the sugar and vanilla extract until just peaking. Spoon a little into the centre of each cake and flatten slightly with the back of the spoon.

3 Arrange the sliced strawberries, overlapping, around the edges of each cake. Halve the reserved strawberries and put a strawberry half in the centre of each cake.

4 Heat the redcurrant jelly in a small heavy-based saucepan with the water until melted, then brush over the strawberries using a pastry brush. Store the cakes in a cool place until ready to serve.

quick tips

• Raspberries will be a delicious alternative to strawberries.

• If you use a fruit such as apricots or nectarines, use strained apricot jam instead of redcurrant jelly to glaze the cakes.

stars, spots and stripes

makes 12

decoration time 20 minutes

½ **quantity Buttercream
(see page 15)**

**12 bought or homemade Fairy Cakes
(see page 13)**

icing sugar or cornflour, for dusting

150 g (5 oz) white ready-to-roll icing

125 g (4 oz) blue ready-to-roll icing

1 Use a small palette knife to spread the buttercream in a thin layer over the tops of the cakes.

2 Dust your work surface with icing sugar or cornflour and knead the ready-to-roll icings, keeping the colours separate. Take 50 g (2 oz) of the white icing, roll it out thinly and cut out 4 circles with a plain 6 cm (2½ inch) biscuit cutter. Use a tiny star-shaped cutter to cut out 6 small stars from each circle. Thinly roll out a little of the blue icing and cut out stars. Fit the blue stars into each white round and carefully transfer to 4 of the cakes.

3 Thinly roll out another 50 g (2 oz) of the white icing. Roll balls of blue icing, about the size of a small pea, between the finger and thumb. Press at intervals on to the white icing. Gently roll the icing with a rolling pin so the blue icing forms dots over the white. Cut out 4 circles with a plain biscuit cutter and transfer to 4 more of the cakes.

4 From the remaining blue and white icing cut out long strips, 5 mm (¼ inch) wide, and lay them together on the work surface to make stripes. Roll lightly with a rolling pin to flatten them and secure together, then cut out 4 more circles. Position them on top of the remaining 4 cakes.

quick tip

• **The same technique of cutting out shapes
from one colour and filling them with the
same shapes cut from a different colour can
be used for numbers, to make these little
cakes suitable for birthday parties.**

butterfly cakes

makes 12

decoration time 15 minutes

**12 bought or homemade Fairy Cakes
(see page 13)**

**single quantity Buttercream
(see page 15)**

1 Use a small, sharp knife to cut out the centre
from each cake and slice each scooped-out
piece in half.

2 Put the buttercream in a big piping bag fitted
with a large star nozzle. Pipe a large swirl of
icing into the hollow of each cake.

3 Reposition the cut-out centres on each cake
at an angle of 45 degrees so they resemble
butterfly wings.

quick tip

• For a special occasion, flavour the buttercream
with chocolate or citrus and dust the cakes
with icing sugar.

piped shell cakes

makes 12

decoration time 30 minutes

200 g (7 oz) icing sugar, plus a little extra

1–2 tablespoons lemon or orange juice

12 bought or homemade Fairy Cakes (see page 13)

½ quantity Buttercream (see page 15)

pink and lilac food colourings

1 Mix the icing sugar in a bowl with 1 tablespoon of the lemon or orange juice. Gradually add the remaining juice, stirring well with a wooden spoon until the icing holds its shape but is not difficult to spread. You might not need all the juice.

2 Reserve 3 tablespoons of the icing and use a small palette knife to spread the remainder over the tops of the cakes. Stir a little extra icing sugar into the reserved icing to thicken it until it just forms peaks when lifted with a knife. Transfer the icing to a piping bag fitted with a writing nozzle.

3 Colour half the buttercream with pink food colouring and the other half with lilac. Transfer the icing to separate piping bags fitted with star nozzles.

4 Pipe rows of pink, lilac and white icing across the cakes.

quick tip

- Children love piping their own designs and personalizing cakes with names or messages. The pink and lilac piping looks pretty on the white background, but you can choose any mixture of colours you like.

3

time to celebrate

first prize

serves 24

decoration time about 1 hour

23 cm (9 inch) square bought or
homemade Basic Sponge Cake
(see page 9)

single quantity Buttercream
(see page 15)

6 tablespoons smooth strawberry or
raspberry jam

45–30 cm (18–12 inch) rectangular
cake board or tray

1.25 kg (2½ lb) white
ready-to-roll icing

icing sugar or cornflour, for dusting

50 g (2 oz) brown ready-to-roll icing

200 g (7 oz) grey ready-to-roll icing

black food colouring

gold food colouring

1 metre (39 inches) red ribbon,
about 3 cm (1¼ inches) wide

red rosette

red ribbon for edges of cake board

1 Slice any dome off the top of the cake. Using a ruler as a guide, cut the cake vertically in half. Cut each half into 3 equal vertical slices and lay the slices together on their sides to make one large rectangle. Cut horizontally through the whole rectangle. Use the buttercream and half the jam to sandwich the cakes together, reassembling them in the rectangle on the board. Spread the remaining jam over the top and sides of the cake.

2 Reserve 200 g (7 oz) of the white icing. Dust your work surface with icing sugar or cornflour and roll out the remainder of the white icing to a rectangle that will cover the cake. Lift it over the cake, easing it down the sides and trimming off the excess around the base.

3 Make the trophy by rolling out the brown icing to a rectangle, 7 x 5 cm (3 x 2 inches), and put it on the top of the cake for the trophy stand, using a dampened paintbrush to secure it in position. Cut out a square of greaseproof paper, 10 x 10 cm (4 x 4 inches), and round off 2 corners to make the shape of a goblet.

4 Roll out a small piece of grey icing and cut out a trophy base, about 5 cm (2 inches) deep and with curved sides. Secure it to the stand. Using the greaseproof paper shape as a template, cut out the goblet shape and secure in position. Roll out the remaining grey icing under the palms of your hands into thin ropes and bend them into handles and trimmings for the trophy base.

5 Lightly knead dots of black food colouring into the reserved white icing to make a marbled effect. Use this to cover the edges of the cake board, trimming off the excess around the edges.

6 Use the gold food colouring to add highlights to the trophy and stand. Secure the ribbon around the sides of the cake and position the rosette beside one of the handles. Secure more ribbon around the edges of the cake board.

quick tips

- Cut the cake into perfectly even thicknesses to make a good base for the icing.

- Serve at a celebration for any sporting triumph – tennis, swimming, golf or horse-riding – and use the appropriate team colours. Paint names or a message on the stand.

graduation cake

serves 20

preparation time 15 minutes

cooking time 1–1¼ hours

decoration time 1 hour

6-egg quantity Basic Sponge Cake mixture (see page 9)

single quantity Buttercream (see page 15)

3 tablespoons smooth apricot jam

250 g (8 oz) ivory-coloured ready-to-roll icing

icing sugar or cornflour, for dusting

1 kg (2 lb) purple ready-to-roll icing

30 x 25 cm (12 x 10 inch) wooden board

50 g (2 oz) yellow ready-to-roll icing

75 g (3 oz) chocolate brown ready-to-roll icing

1 tube yellow writing icing

gold food colouring

1 Turn the cake mixture into a greased and lined cake tin, 23 cm (9 inches) square. Bake in a preheated oven, 160°C (325°F), Gas Mark 3, for 1–1¼ hours until just firm and a skewer inserted into the centre comes out clean. Leave to cool. Slice any dome off the top of the cake. Cut a slice, 5 cm (2 inches) wide, off one side and position it at one end of the larger piece. Trim off the excess to make a rectangle. Cut the cake in half horizontally and sandwich the layers with the buttercream, securing the smaller piece of cake to the larger one with more buttercream.

2 Use a sharp knife to round off the corners of one long side. Cut curves into the other long side and the ends to make a book shape. Spread the 3 curved sides with a little jam. Reserve a little of the ivory-coloured icing. Dust your work surface with icing sugar or cornflour and roll out the remainder of the icing to a long strip the depth of the cake and the length of the 3 sides. Press it into position and score it with a knife.

3 Roll out a scant half of the purple icing to a rectangle about 1 cm (½ inch) longer and 1 cm (½ inch) wider than the cake. Put it on the board and position the cake on top so that the ivory-coloured icing sits about 5 mm (¼ inch) away from the edges of the purple icing. Roll out the remaining purple icing to the same length but add an extra 5 cm (2 inches) to the width to cover the 'spine' of the book. Position it on the cake, tucking the ends under the spine.

4 Use the reserved ivory-coloured icing to make the owl's head and body and secure to the cake with a dampened paintbrush. Use the yellow icing for eyes and claws and the brown icing for wings, the top of the head, the beak and centres of the eyes. Position 2 more rectangles of brown icing on the spine. Pipe yellow icing around the edges and spine and around the owl's wings. Dab spots of gold food colouring on the owl's breast.

quick tip

- Purple icing can be made by kneading Grape Violet food colouring into white icing or by kneading together red and blue icings.

bon voyage

serves 20

decoration time 30 minutes

23 cm (9 inch) square bought or
homemade Basic Sponge Cake
(see page 9)

single quantity Buttercream
(see page 15)

large metal tray or 28 cm (11 inch)
square cake board

3 tablespoons smooth apricot jam

icing sugar or cornflour, for dusting

1 kg (2 lb) dark red
ready-to-roll icing

200 g (7 oz) white ready-to-roll icing

silver food colouring

1 Slice any dome off the top of the cake. Cut a slice 8 cm (3¼ inches) wide off the cake and then cut off (and discard) one-third of the slice to leave 2 rectangular pieces. Halve each horizontally and sandwich the layers with buttercream. Put the larger cake on the tray or board and brush both cakes with apricot jam.

2 Dust your work surface with icing sugar or cornflour and roll out two-thirds of the red icing to a rectangle, 10 cm (4 inches) longer and wider than the large cake. Lay the icing over the cake, smoothing the icing down the sides and trimming off the excess around the base. Cover the small cake with the remaining red icing and put it on the large cake.

3 Roll out a thin strip of white icing and trim it to a strip 1 cm (½ inch) wide and long enough to go around the small cake. Lightly dampen the back of the strip and secure it in position. Use a larger strip to wrap around the large cake. Run the tip of a knife along each strip to make an indentation. Cut out small rectangles of icing and position 2 rectangles on the small case at either side of the strip and 2 on the large case. Add smaller rectangles of icing for the clasps.

4 Roll 2 pieces of icing, each 40 g (1½ oz), into sausage shapes and bend the ends over to shape handles. Secure them in position. Paint the clasps with silver food colouring.

quick tips

- If you're throwing a large party for someone about to set off on their travels, you could use a rich fruit cake instead of a sponge cake. If you do, cover it with almond paste before icing (see page 21).

- As a finishing touch, write the recipient's name and destination on a luggage label and attach it to one of the handles.

welcome home

serves 40

decoration time 1 hour

25 cm (10 inch) round Rich Fruit Cake, covered with almond paste (see pages 11 and 21 for recipe and technique)

30 cm (12 inch) round cake board

icing sugar or cornflour, for dusting

1 kg (2 lb) white ready-to-roll icing

75 g (3 oz) each of orange, chocolate brown, green, red and blue ready-to-roll icing

1 tube red writing icing

red ribbon for edge of cake board

1 Put the cake on the board. Dust your work surface with icing sugar or cornflour and roll out the white icing to a circle, 38 cm (15 inches) across. Lay it over the cake, smoothing the icing around the sides and trimming off the excess around the base.

2 Roll out a little of the orange icing and trim to a rectangle, 12 x 7 cm (5 x 2¾ inches). Dampen the underside lightly with water and put it on top of the cake. Roll out the brown icing and cut out 2 strips, 5 mm (¼ inch) wide and each the width of the orange rectangle. Position one strip at each end of the orange icing. Cut out 2 further rectangles, 17 x 3 cm (6½ x 1¼ inches), from the brown icing. Lay them against the long sides of the orange icing and trim off the ends at angles to represent open doors. Cut out windows in the top half of the doors and add 2 doorknobs.

3 Pipe scallops of red writing icing around the sides of the cake and at the top of the doors. Thinly roll out a little orange, green, red and blue icing and cut them into strips 2 cm (¾ inch) wide. From each strip cut out triangles for bunting. Dampen the pieces with water and secure them to the cake. Use red icing to cover the edges of the cake board.

4 Shape a small case in blue icing and put it on top of the cake next to the open doors. Write a message on the bunting if liked and secure the red ribbon around the edge of the board.

quick tips

- Use the writing icing tube to write a message – the recipient's name or 'Welcome', for example – on the bunting on top of the cake.

- If you're not used to writing with icing, practise on a sheet of greaseproof paper.

new parents

serves 24

decoration time 1 hour

**15 cm (6 inch) and 20 cm (8 inch)
round bought or homemade Basic
Sponge Cakes (see page 9)**

**double quantity Buttercream
(see page 15)**

8 tablespoons lemon or orange curd

**25–28 cm (10–11 inch) round or
square plate**

icing sugar or cornflour, for dusting

**1.3 kg (2¾ lb) pale pink or blue
ready-to-roll icing**

**25 g (1 oz) flesh-coloured
ready-to-roll icing**

**50 g (2 oz) dark pink or blue
ready-to-roll icing**

blue food colouring

50 g (2 oz) white ready-to-roll icing

50 g (2 oz) yellow ready-to-roll icing

**small plastic cake decorations
(e.g., nappy pins, rattles)**

**50 g (2 oz) small pink and yellow
soft sweets**

1 Cut each cake in half horizontally and sandwich the layers together with half the buttercream and the lemon or orange curd. Spread the remaining buttercream over the top and sides of the cakes. Put the larger cake on the plate.

2 Dust your work surface with icing sugar or cornflour and roll out two-thirds of the pink or blue icing to a circle, 33 cm (13 inches) across, and cover the larger cake, smoothing the icing down the sides and trimming off the excess around the base. Roll out the remaining icing to a circle, 28 cm (11 inches) across, and cover the smaller cake. Position the smaller cake on the centre of the larger one.

3 Roll a small ball of flesh-coloured icing for baby's head, adding a small button nose. Shape hands and feet with more flesh-coloured icing. Roll the dark pink or blue icing into an oval and flatten it slightly with the palm of your hand. Make 2 cuts for the arms and one for the legs. Smooth out the edges and cut off the tips. Make button markings with the tip of a paintbrush. Secure the baby to the top of the cake with a dampened paintbrush, bending the shape into a sitting-up position.

4 Secure the head, hands and feet and add features with the blue colouring and a fine paintbrush.

5 Shape feeding bottles from the remaining icing and secure them around the cake with the plastic cake decorations. Scatter plenty of small sweets around the tiers.

quick tip

• This makes a fabulous gift for new parents, who can indulge in it themselves or serve it to the stream of visitors who'll come to admire their baby. It would also make a good christening cake if you're looking for something a bit different.

first night

serves 24

decoration time 1 hour, plus drying

icing sugar or cornflour, for dusting

1.25 kg (2½ lb) white
ready-to-roll icing

25 cm (10 inch) round bought or
homemade Basic Sponge Cake
(see page 9)

single quantity Buttercream
(see page 15)

6 tablespoons raspberry or
strawberry jam

30–35 cm (12–14 inch) round plate,
preferably gold or red

425 g (14 oz) red ready-to-roll icing

50 cm (20 inches) fine red cord

50 cm (20 inches) fine gold cord

50 g (2 oz) purple ready-to-roll icing

gold food colouring

1 Wrap a piece of nonstick baking paper around a tall tumbler and prop it up at either side with a little icing. To make the mask templates cut out 2 rectangles, each 10 x 7 cm (4 x 3 inches), from greaseproof paper and fold them in half lengthways. Round off the lower half of the masks from halfway along the sides to the point of the folded edge. Gently curve the top edge of the masks from the folded point to the sides. Cut out eyes. Cut a smiling mouth on one mask and a sad mouth on the other.

2 Dust your work surface with icing sugar or cornflour and roll out 100 g (3½ oz) of the white icing. Lay the templates over the icing and cut out the mask shapes. Carefully transfer them to the tumbler so they set in a curved shape. Leave them for 24 hours.

3 Cut the cake in half horizontally and sandwich the layers with half the buttercream and all the jam. Put it on the plate and spread the top and sides with the remaining buttercream.

4 Roll out the remaining white icing to a circle, 35 cm (14 inches) across, and cover the cake, smoothing the icing around the sides and trimming off the excess around the base.

5 Halve the red icing and thinly roll one half to a rectangle, about 28 x 12 cm (11 x 5 inches). Drape the icing over one side of the cake, pinching it together slightly in the centre to resemble curtains. Use a dampened paintbrush to secure the red icing to the white so it doesn't slip. Secure 2 lengths of cord around the icing then make the other curtain in the same way. Cut out thin strips of purple icing, about 5 mm (¼ inch) wide, and secure them around the edges of the curtains.

6 Carefully peel the paper away from the masks and paint them gold. Position them, slightly overlapping, on top of the cake.

quick tip

• This is a brilliant cake for budding actors. The masks are far easier to make than they look and can be made well in advance so they have plenty of time to harden. Make a spare one of each – just in case of breakages.

winter wedding cake

serves 50–55

decoration time 1 hour, plus drying

15 cm (6 inch) and 25 cm (10 inch)
round bought or homemade Rich
Fruit Cakes, covered with almond
paste (see pages 11 and 21 for
recipe and technique)

35–40 cm (14–16 inch) round glass
plate or cake stand

double quantity Royal Icing
(see page 18)

1 egg white, lightly beaten

12 rosemary sprigs, about 6 cm
(2½ inches) long

8 bay leaf sprigs

caster and icing sugar, for dusting

8 small fir cones

100 g (3½ oz) sugar cubes

6 tea lights

1 Put the larger cake on the plate and spread two-thirds of the royal icing over it, swirling it in an even layer with a palette knife. Put the smaller cake on top and cover it with the remaining icing.

2 To frost the herb sprigs, put the lightly beaten egg white in a bowl. Use your fingers to coat a rosemary sprig with egg white so that it's evenly moistened but not dripping. Dip the sprig into caster sugar and transfer it to a tray covered with nonstick baking paper. Leave it to dry for at least 1 hour. Coat the remaining rosemary and the bay leaf sprigs in the same way.

3 Using a tea strainer, generously dust the fir cones with icing sugar. Put the sugar cubes into a plastic bag and tap them gently with a rolling pin until they are broken into smaller pieces.

4 Dust the plate with icing sugar. Position 2 tea lights on the top tier and 4 on the lower tier. Arrange the herbs and fir cones around the tea lights and scatter the pieces of sugar to fill the gaps between the decorations and around the lower tier. Cover loosely and store in a cool place for up to 1 week.

quick tip

• This cake will make a great centrepiece for your Christmas table or for a winter wedding anniversary or birthday party. Don't forget to light the tea lights for a truly stunning effect!

white chocolate wedding cake

serves 30–35

decoration time 1½ hours

400 g (13 oz) white chocolate

25 g (1 oz) unsalted butter

15 cm (6 inch) and 25 cm (10 inch) round bought or homemade Rich Chocolate Cakes (see page 10)

30–35 cm (12–14 inch) round glass or frosted glass plate

triple quantity White Chocolate Ganache (see page 17)

12–14 white freesias

8–10 white or coral pink ranunculus

6–8 white or cream-coloured lisianthus

1 Break the white chocolate into pieces and put them in a bowl with the butter. Place the bowl over a saucepan of gently simmering water and leave it until the chocolate has melted. Gently stir the chocolate to incorporate the butter. Tip the mixture on to a piece of marble or glass or a thoroughly clean plastic chopping board and spread it to a thin, even layer. Leave in a cool place or in the refrigerator until set.

2 When the chocolate is just set, draw a fine-bladed knife across it at an angle of 45 degrees to pare off long chocolate curls. If the chocolate breaks off in brittle shavings it's too cold, so leave it at room temperature for a few minutes and try again. If the chocolate is sticky and clings to the knife put it in the refrigerator for about 10 minutes and then try again.

3 Put the larger cake on the plate and spread two-thirds of the ganache over it. While the ganache is still soft press the chocolate curls vertically into it. You needn't be too precise or careful about doing this – the more casually it's done, the better the finished result.

4 Position the small cake on top of the larger one and cover it with the remaining ganache. Press more chocolate curls around the sides. Keep the cake in a cool place or in the refrigerator until ready to serve.

5 Cut the stems of all the flowers short and use them to decorate the tops of the cakes.

quick tips

- Chocolate curls – caraque – are stunning cake decorations and are easy to make once you've got the hang of the technique. Make them a couple of weeks in advance and keep them in a cool place or in the refrigerator until you need them.

- The day before the wedding, complete the cake up to the end of step 4, leaving only the flowers to arrange on the day.

chocolate wedding cake

serves 34

decoration time 1½ hours

15 cm (6 inch) round and 25 cm (10 inch) round bought or homemade Rich Chocolate Cakes (see page 10)

triple quantity Chocolate Fudge Icing (see page 18)

20 cm (8 inch), 30 cm (12 inch), 33 cm (13 inch) and 35 cm (14 inch) round cake boards

icing sugar or cornflour, for dusting

2 kg (4 lb) chocolate brown ready-to-roll icing

1.5 metres (5 feet) coffee-coloured ribbon, 4 cm (1½ inches) wide

4 metres (13 feet) white ribbon for edges of cake boards

500 g (1 lb) box of chocolates

100 g (3½ oz) mixed chocolate coffee beans

1 Cut both cakes in half horizontally and sandwich the layers together with half the chocolate fudge icing. Put the smaller cake on the 20 cm (8 inch) board and the larger cake on the 30 cm (12 inch) board. Spread the top and sides of the cakes with the remaining icing.

2 Dust your work surface with icing sugar or cornflour and roll out 1 kg (2 lb) of the icing to a circle, 35 cm (14 inches) across. Lift the icing over the larger cake. Smooth the icing down the sides and trim off the excess around the base. Reserve the trimmings.

3 Roll out a further 750 g (1½ lb) of the icing and use it to cover the smaller cake. Knead the trimmings and remaining icing together. Secure the 2 largest cake boards together with clear adhesive tape, then secure the large cake, on its board, on top.

4 Cover all the top edges of the cake boards with the remaining icing, starting with the smallest and working down to the largest board. Rest the smaller cake on top of the larger one. Wrap the coffee-coloured ribbon around the cakes. Secure the ivory-coloured ribbon around all the boards.

5 Pile the chocolates on top of the smaller cake and around the edge of the larger one. Scatter the coffee beans on top.

quick tip

- If you're transporting this cake to a special event keep the tiers separate until you get there and assemble the cake in its final position, scattering over the chocolates and coffee beans at the last minute.

ribbony chocolate wedding cake

serves 50

decoration time 1 hour, plus standing

15 cm (6 inch), 20 cm (8 inch) and 25 cm (10 inch) round bought or homemade Rich Chocolate Cakes (see page 10)

triple quantity Dark Chocolate Ganache (see page 17)

30 cm (12 inch) round cake stand or glass plate

3 metres (10 feet) wired red ribbon, about 4 cm (1½ inches) wide

3 metres (10 feet) wired lilac or cream-coloured ribbon, about 2.5 cm (1 inch) wide

about 20 small, dried, red, pale green, lilac or cream-coloured flowers

1 Cut each cake in half horizontally and use about a quarter of the ganache to sandwich the layers together.

2 Put the largest cake on the cake stand or plate and cover it with a scant half of the ganache, swirling it in an even layer with a palette knife. Rest the medium-sized cake on top and spread with more ganache. Position the smallest cake on top and spread with the remaining ganache. Leave the cake in a cool place for about 1 hour until the chocolate has firmed up slightly.

3 Wrap the red ribbon around your hand and then uncoil it loosely around the cake, starting at the top and working around the cake in a spiral to the bottom. Pressing the edge of the ribbon gently into the chocolate icing on the top tier should be sufficient to hold it in place. It can then be secured under the edge of the cake stand at the other end with a small piece of clear adhesive tape.

4 Create the same effect with the narrower ribbon, keeping the coil loose and informal.

5 Tuck the flowers, in groups of 2–3, among the coils of ribbon decoration.

quick tips

- Before covering the cake layers with ganache, drizzle them with an orange or coffee liqueur or with brandy. Allow about 4 tablespoons for the top tier, 100 ml (3½ fl oz) for the middle tier and 150 ml (¼ pint) for the bottom tier.

- If you want to make the cake in advance, assemble it to the end of step 2 and store overnight in a cool place. Add the flowers and ribbons the following day.

layered rose wedding cake

serves 75–80

decoration time 1½ hours

12 cm (5 inch), 18 cm (7 inch) and
23 cm (9 inch) square bought or
homemade Rich Fruit Cakes, covered
with almond paste (see pages 11 and
21 for recipe and technique)

15 cm (6 inch), 20 cm (8 inch) and
28 cm (11 inch) square cake boards,
plus 3 x 12 cm (5 inch) and
3 x 18 cm (7 inch) round boards
for stacking

icing sugar or cornflour, for dusting

2.25 kg (5 lb) ivory-coloured
ready-to-roll icing

3 metres (10 feet) ivory-coloured
ribbon for edges of boards

about 30 pale pink or 30
ivory-coloured open roses or a
mixture of the 2 colours

small posy of roses for top of cake

1 Put the cakes on the square boards. Dust your work surface with icing sugar or cornflour and roll out 1 kg (2 lb) of the icing to a 35 cm (14 inch) square. Lift the icing over the largest cake. Smooth it down the sides and trim off the excess around the base.

2 Cover the medium-sized cake with 750g (1½ lb) of the icing and the small cake with the remainder, each time rolling the icing to a square 12 cm (5 inches) larger than the diameter of the cake.

3 Use clear adhesive tape to fasten together the 12 cm (5 inch) boards and the 18 cm (7 inch) boards. Secure the ivory-coloured ribbon around the edges of the boards.

4 To assemble the cake put the 18 cm (7 inch) stacked cake boards on the large cake and position the medium-sized cake on top. Put the 12 cm (5 inch) stacked cake boards on top of this and position the small cake on top.

5 Cut the rose stems down to 2 cm (¾ inch). Tuck all the roses, closely together, around the 2 bottom tiers, fitting them together so they make an attractive decoration without looking too crammed. Arrange the posy of roses on top of the cake.

quick tip

• This cake can be prepared up to the end of step 4 several weeks in advance, but the assembly of the roses needs to be done on the day. Set the posy in a shallow bowl of water and wrap the ends of the other roses in moistened cotton wool, then in foil or clingfilm so the water does not seep out over the cake.

sugared almond wedding cake

serves 20

decoration time 30 minutes

18 cm (7 inch) square homemade
Rich Fruit Cake (see page 11) or
3 bought fruit slab cakes

4 tablespoons smooth apricot jam

25 cm (10 inch) square or 30 cm
(12 inch) round cake plate
or cake stand

icing sugar or cornflour, for dusting

1.5 kg (3 lb) white ready-to-roll icing

18 cm (7 inch) square silver
cake board

1 kg (2 lb) white or coloured
sugared almonds

2 metres (6 feet) wired ribbon, about
5 cm (2 inches) wide

silver, pink or white wedding confetti

1 Spread the top and sides of the cake with the apricot jam. If you are using bought cakes, secure them together with a little of the jam to make a deep, square cake. Put the cake on the plate or cake stand.

2 Dust your work surface with icing sugar or cornflour and knead the icing to soften it slightly. Roll out 200 g (7 oz) to an 18 cm (7 inch) square, and lay it on top of the cake. Reserve 250 g (9 oz) of the remaining icing and roll out the remainder to a rectangle, 30 x 20 cm (12 x 8 inches). From this cut out 4 rectangles, each 18 cm (7 inches) long and 1 cm (½ inch) deeper than the cake. Make sure that all 4 rectangles are the same length and depth. Secure a rectangle to each cake side, pinching them together at the corners to secure.

3 Dampen the top and sides of the cake board with water. Roll out the remaining icing to a 23 cm (9 inch) square and use it to cover the board, folding the icing down the sides and pinching it together at the corners. Trim off the excess around the base and at the corners.

4 Scatter the sugared almonds into the top of the cake and carefully balance the icing-covered 'lid' in position. Cut the ribbon into 4 even lengths. Use the tip of a knife to ease one end of each length under each side of the cake. Bring the loose ends up over the top of the cake and fasten them together in a loose bow. Scatter the base with the confetti.

quick tips

- Don't forget to drizzle the cake with a few tablespoons of brandy or liqueur before decorating.

- You might want to cover the cake with 1 kg (2 lb) almond paste (see page 21) before covering it with icing.

fruit and flowers

serves 24

decoration time 30 minutes

25 cm (10 inch) round bought or homemade Rich Fruit Cake, covered with almond paste (see pages 11 and 21 for recipe and technique)

30 cm (12 inch) round white or red plate

icing sugar or cornflour, for dusting

1 kg (2 lb) white ready-to-roll icing

500 g (1 lb) red fruits (e.g., strawberries, blackberries, clusters of red grapes, raspberries)

3 large open red roses

1.5 metres (5 feet) red ribbon, about 4 cm (1½ inches) wide

1 Put the cake on the plate. Dust your work surface with icing sugar or cornflour and roll out the icing to a circle, 38 cm (15 inches) across. Lay it over the cake, smooth the icing around the sides and trim off the excess.

2 Pile the fruits on top of the cake, starting with the larger ones and clusters of grapes.

3 Tuck the roses in among the fruits. Secure the ribbon around the sides of the cake, finishing with a bow if liked. Use a fine tea strainer to dust the fruit and flowers with icing sugar.

quick tips

- One of the easiest and most effective cakes to decorate, this idea is perfect for a novice to cake decorating to practise their skills.

- The cake is ideal for a wedding anniversary, particularly a ruby wedding.

- The cake can be iced a couple of weeks in advance and the fruits and flowers added at the last minute. Make sure the fruits are dry before you arrange them on the icing, otherwise the juices will make the icing soften and the sugar dusting will dissolve.

silver wedding cake

serves 40

decoration time 1½ hours

25 cm (10 inch) round bought or homemade Rich Fruit Cake, covered with almond paste (see pages 11 and 21 for recipe and technique)

35 cm (14 inch) round cake board

icing sugar or cornflour, for dusting

1.25 kg (2½ lb) white ready-to-roll icing

small 2 and 5 cutters

2 sheets or 1 small tub edible silver leaf

5 silver or white candles

1.5 metres (5 feet) coloured ribbon, about 4 cm (1½ inches) wide

white ribbon for edge of cake board

about 15 silver sugared almonds

1 Put the cake on the board. Reserve 200 g (7 oz) of the icing. Dust your work surface with icing sugar or cornflour and roll out the remainder of the icing to a circle, 38 cm (15 inches) across. Lift the icing over the cake and smooth it around the sides, trimming off the excess around the base. Use the reserved icing to cover the cake board, trimming off the excess around the edges.

2 Thinly roll out the icing trimmings and cut out 3 each of the numbers 2 and 5. Set aside on a sheet of greaseproof paper.

3 Use a pair of tweezers to tear a little silver leaf from the sheet or tub. Hold it over the cake, about 5 cm (2 inches) away from the edge. Lightly dampen the surface of the cake where the silver is to be applied and then lower it into position, smoothing it down with a dry brush.

4 Arrange 3 number 25s on the cake, spacing them evenly apart and each about 5 cm (2 inches) from the edge, and fill up the areas between them with additional silver leaf. Apply more areas of silver leaf to the cake board.

5 Position the candles on top of the cake and secure the ribbon around the sides, finishing in a bow. Secure the white ribbon to the edge of the board. Scatter the sugared almonds in clusters over the cake and board.

quick tip

• Although silver leaf might seem difficult to use at first, you'll quickly get used to it after applying a few pieces. Because it's almost weightless, make sure you work in a draught-free area so that it doesn't blow away before you've had a chance to secure it to the cake!

golden wedding cake

serves 40

decoration time 1 hour

25 cm (10 inch) round bought or homemade Rich Fruit Cake (see page 11)

18 cm (7 inch) round cake board

4 tablespoons smooth apricot jam

icing sugar or cornflour, for dusting

2 kg (4 lb) almond paste

30 cm (12 inch) round cake stand or glass plate

2 kg (4 lb) white ready-to-roll icing

2.5 metres (8 feet) gold ribbon, 3–4 cm (1¼–1½ inches) wide

10 gold-coloured roses

plain glass tumbler, about 15 cm (6 inches) tall and at least 8 cm (3¼ inches) in diameter

1 Remove the cake centre (see tip). Put the removed centre on the cake board. Brush the top and sides of both cakes with jam.

2 Measure the inner circumference of the ring cake with string. Dust your work surface with icing sugar or cornflour and roll out a little of the almond paste. Trim it to a strip, the length of the string and the depth of the cake. Roll up the strip and unroll it in the centre of the cake, pressing it firmly in position.

3 Reserve 400 g (13 oz) of the almond paste. Roll out the remainder to a circle, 38 cm (15 inches) across, and cut out a circle in the centre, using the small dish as a template. Lift the paste over the cake so that the cut-out centre lines up with the hole in the cake. Fit the paste around the sides and trim off the excess around the base. Transfer to the cake stand or plate.

4 Lightly knead the trimmings into the remaining paste and roll to a circle, 25 cm (10 inches) across. Lay the paste over the small cake, easing it to fit around the sides. Trim off the excess.

5 Use the white icing to cover both cakes, using the same technique as for the almond paste.

6 Secure the gold ribbon around the cakes, finishing with a bow on the bottom tier. Pour a little water into the tumbler and arrange several of the roses in it, cutting the stems to varying heights. Put it inside the ring cake. Use rose petals and more roses to decorate the tops of both cakes. Position the small cake over the glass tumbler.

quick tip

- To remove the centre of the cake invert a dish with a diameter of 12 cm (5 inches) on the centre of the cake. Holding a knife vertically, cut out the centre of the cake and remove it carefully.

champagne bottle

serves 15

decoration time 1 hour

icing sugar or cornflour, for dusting

300 g (10 oz) grey ready-to-roll icing

35 x 25 cm (14 x 10 inch) rectangular cake board

2 bought or homemade Swiss Rolls (see page 12)

single quantity Buttercream (see page 15)

500 g (1 lb) dark green ready-to-roll icing

75 g (3 oz) black ready-to-roll icing

50 g (2 oz) white ready-to-roll icing

black and gold food colouring

dark green ribbon for edges of cake board

1 Dust your work surface with icing sugar or cornflour and thinly roll out the grey icing to a rectangle that will cover the cake board. Trim off the excess around the base.

2 Put the Swiss rolls on the work surface, end to end, and cut them down to an overall length of 30 cm (12 inches). Cut a 'neck' out of one end, trimming off the cut edges to make a curved bottle shape. Use a little buttercream to sandwich the join in the cakes, then spread a thin layer over the cakes.

3 Roll out a little of the green icing and cut an oval, the same diameter as the base of the bottle. Press it into position. Roll out the remaining green icing and use it to cover the rest of the bottle, smoothing it to fit over the neck of the bottle and trimming off the excess around the base. Use a fish slice to transfer the cake to the board, supporting it carefully under the join.

4 Roll out the black icing and use it to decorate the top of the bottle. Use the white icing and the black icing trimmings to shape the labels.

5 Use a fine paintbrush to decorate the bottle with the black and gold food colourings. Secure the ribbon around the board.

quick tip

• If you're using a bought Swiss roll you might need to buy an extra one and add an additional layer because they tend to be much thinner than homemade ones.

individual wedding cakes

makes 12

decoration time 20 minutes

12 bought or homemade Fairy Cakes (see page 13)

4 tablespoons sherry or orange-flavoured liqueur (optional)

200 g (7 oz) icing sugar, sifted

1–2 tablespoons lemon juice

36 sugared almonds

12 frosted flowers

fine white ribbon, to decorate

1 Drizzle the cakes with the liqueur, if using. Mix the icing sugar in a bowl with 1 tablespoon of the lemon juice. Gradually add the remaining lemon juice, stirring well with a wooden spoon until the icing holds its shape but is not difficult to spread – you might not need all the juice.

2 Use a small palette knife to spread the lemon-flavoured icing over the tops of the cakes. Arrange 3 sugared almonds in the centre of each cake.

3 Arrange a frosted flower on top of each cake and tie a length of white ribbon around each cake case to decorate it, finishing with a bow.

quick tips

- To frost flowers, lightly whisk an egg white in a small bowl. Put about 100 g (3½ oz) caster sugar in another bowl. Either dip a flower into the egg white or use a large paintbrush to coat the petals, then sprinkle the flower generously with sugar until it is evenly coated. Transfer the flowers to a sheet of baking parchment and leave in a cool place for at least 1 hour to dry.

- These little cakes are perfect for a country-style family wedding. You could add guests' name tags to them and place them around the dining table. Choose sugared almonds to suit the colour scheme of the wedding. If you are using ribbon, secure it around the paper cases before you begin decorating.

4

seasonal cakes

red heart cake

serves 50–55

decoration time 1 hour

12 cm (5 inch) and 23 cm (9 inch)
square bought or homemade
Rich Fruit Cakes, covered with
almond paste (see pages 11 and 21
for recipe and technique)

28 cm (11 inch) square cake board

icing sugar or cornflour, for dusting

1.5 kg (3 lb) white ready-to-roll icing

heart-shaped biscuit cutters in
2 or 3 sizes

2 metres (6 feet) red ribbon, about
4 cm (1½ inches) wide

red ribbon for edges of cake board

small glass dish, about 5 cm
(2 inches) in diameter

15–20 red foil-wrapped,
heart-shaped chocolates

1 Put the larger cake on the board. Dust your work surface with icing sugar or cornflour and roll out 1 kg (2 lb) of the icing to a 35 cm (14 inch) square. Lift the icing over the cake, smooth the icing down the sides and trim off the excess around the base.

2 Use the remaining icing to cover the smaller cake. Position it over the larger cake, about 2 cm (¾ inch) from one edge. Reserve the icing trimmings.

3 While the icing is still soft, gently press the cutters into the surface so they leave an impression when lifted away. If the cutters start to stick to the icing, dip them in a little icing sugar before impressing each shape. Cover the edges of the board with the icing trimmings.

4 Secure the ribbon around the cakes, finishing the top tier with a bow. Secure more ribbon around the cake board. Fill the glass bowl with chocolates and put it on top of the cake. Scatter more chocolates over both tiers.

quick tips

- This cake is perfect for an unconventional wedding or a St Valentine's Day party.

- If you use a basic sponge cake instead of rich fruit cake you do not need the layer of almond paste.

be my valentine

serves 6–8

decoration time 30 minutes, plus chilling

12–15 cm (5–6 inch) round bought or homemade Rich Chocolate Cake (see page 10)

single quantity White Chocolate Ganache (see page 17)

pink, lilac or cream-coloured plate

200 g (7 oz) white chocolate

pink or lilac food colouring paste

handful of small heart-shaped sweets

1 Cut the cake in half horizontally and sandwich the layers with a little of the ganache. Put it on the plate and spread the top and sides with the remaining ganache, swirling it in an even layer with a small palette knife.

2 Measure the circumference of the cake with a piece of string. Cut a strip of greaseproof paper 2 cm (¾ inch) longer than the string and 5 cm (2 inches) deeper than the cake.

3 Break the chocolate into pieces and melt them in a bowl set over a pan of gently simmering water. Spoon half the chocolate on to the strip of greaseproof paper. Spread it to the edge of one long side and to 1 cm (½ inch) from both short ends. On the other long side of the strip use a thick paintbrush or pastry brush to spread the chocolate to the edges in an uneven, jagged line. Return the chocolate in the bowl to the pan, but turn off the heat so the remaining chocolate stays melted over the warm water.

4 Leave the chocolate strip to cool slightly, but do not allow it to set. Carefully wrap it around the cake (paper side outwards) so that the jagged edge is uppermost. Chill for about 30 minutes until the chocolate is brittle.

5 Meanwhile, spoon 2 tablespoons of the remaining chocolate into a small bowl and beat in a dot of food colouring paste. Transfer it to a paper piping bag and snip off the tip. Pipe about 12 heart shapes on to a sheet of greaseproof paper. Use a small teaspoon to fill the centre of each heart with the remaining chocolate, nudging it gently to the edges. Chill for 30 minutes.

6 Carefully peel away the paper from the cake. Once the chocolate hearts have set, peel away the paper and arrange the hearts on top of the cake. Scatter with the heart sweets.

quick tip

- Make sure you use food colouring paste for the decoration because liquid colour will make the chocolate solidify.

mother's day cake

serves 12

decoration time 45 minutes,
plus drying

1 egg white

75 g (3 oz) caster sugar

**about 25 red, pink and
yellow primroses**

**18 cm (7 inch) round bought or
homemade Basic Sponge Cake
(see page 9)**

150 g (5 oz) lemon curd

**20 cm (8 inch) round or square
cream-coloured plate**

**double quantity Buttercream
(see page 15)**

1 Lightly whisk the egg white in a small bowl
with 1 tablespoon of water until it is broken up.
Put the sugar in a separate bowl. Gently pull
one of the flowers away from its calyx. Using a
paintbrush or your fingers, lightly coat each side
of the petals in egg white. Sprinkle with caster
sugar until completely coated. Transfer the
flower, face down, to a sheet of nonstick baking
paper or greaseproof paper. If the flower starts
to fall flat, losing its shape, support it on a tiny
crumpled ball of greaseproof paper. Frost the
remaining flowers in the same way and leave
them to dry for at least 1 hour or overnight.

2 Cut the cake horizontally into three and
sandwich the layers together with lemon curd.
Put the cake on the plate.

3 Spread a thin layer of buttercream over the
top and sides of the cake to seal in the crumbs.
Spread the remaining buttercream over the
cake, smoothing it out with a palette knife.
Arrange the frosted flowers around the top
edges of the cake.

quick tip

• Frosted flowers keep well for several weeks if
stored in an airtight container. Make sure
they're completely dry first, then arrange them
in layers, interleaving each with kitchen paper.

chocolate egg cake

serves 10

decoration time 30 minutes

100 g (3½ oz) milk chocolate

200 g (7 oz) plain chocolate

150 ml (¼ pint) double cream

18 cm (7 inch) bought or homemade Rich Chocolate Cake (see page 10)

23–25 cm (9–10 inch) round, flat plate

selection of plain, milk or white chocolate eggs

1 Break the milk chocolate into pieces and melt them in a bowl set over a pan of gently simmering water. Line a baking sheet with nonstick baking paper or greaseproof paper. Use a teaspoon to scribble the melted chocolate in irregular lines all over the paper. Don't try to be neat – the more casual the lines are, the better they'll be. Put the chocolate in the refrigerator for 20 minutes.

2 Chop the plain chocolate. Heat 100 ml (3½ fl oz) of the cream in a small heavy-based saucepan until it is bubbling around the edges but not boiling. Remove from the heat and stir in the chocolate. Turn the mixture into a bowl and stir until it is melted and smooth. Stir in the remaining cream.

3 Cut the cake in half horizontally and sandwich the layers with a little of the chocolate cream. Put the cake on the plate and tip the remaining chocolate cream over the top, spreading it with a palette knife so it covers the sides in swirls.

4 Take the milk chocolate shapes from the refrigerator and peel away the nonstick baking paper or greaseproof paper. Break the chocolate into long, irregular pieces. Scatter them over the cake and pile the eggs on top. Keep the cake in a cool place until ready to serve.

quick tip

- If the cream boils in the pan, remove it from the heat and let it cool a little before you add the chocolate. It'll take a little longer to thicken so that it can be spread over the cake, so keep an eye on it as it cools.

easter egg

serves 8–10

preparation time 15 minutes,
plus cooling

cooking time 1–1¼ hours

decoration time 30 minutes

3-egg quantity Rich Chocolate Cake
(see page 10)

300 g (10 oz) chocolate
hazelnut spread

icing sugar or cornflour, for dusting

500 g (1 lb) chocolate brown
ready-to-roll icing

50 g (2 oz) milk chocolate

oval plate, about 28 cm
(11 inches) long

1.5 metres (5 feet) ribbon, about
4 cm (1½ inches) wide

1 Grease a 2.5 litre (4 pint) ovenproof basin and line the base with a circle of greaseproof paper. Turn the cake mixture into the basin and level the surface. Bake in a preheated oven, 180°C (350°F), Gas Mark 4, for 1–1¼ hours or until the cake feels just firm in the centre. Leave to cool in the basin.

2 Run a knife around the edges of the basin and invert the cake on a board. To make the egg shape, start by cutting a vertical slice, 5 cm (2 inches) wide, off 2 opposite sides of the cake. Keeping the knife vertical, cut away more of the cake at one end to make a pointed egg shape, then round off all the edges of the cake, remembering that the cake will be shallower at the pointed end than at the thick end. Keep the trimmings. Slice the egg shape vertically into 3 layers and sandwich them together with a little of the chocolate spread. Cover the egg with the remaining chocolate spread.

3 Dust your work surface with icing sugar or cornflour and roll out the icing to an oval, 33 x 28 cm (13 x 11 inches). Lift the icing over the cake and smooth it to fit around the sides. Trim off the excess around the base. Transfer the cake to a tray or board lined with nonstick baking paper or greaseproof paper.

4 Break the chocolate into pieces and put them in a bowl over a pan of gently simmering water until the chocolate has melted. Put the chocolate in a paper piping bag and snip off the tip. Using a scribbling action, pipe lines of chocolate diagonally across the egg. Use a fish slice to transfer the cake to the serving plate. Keep it in a cool place until the chocolate has set.

5 Use the tip of a knife to tuck one end of the ribbon under the end of the egg. Wrap the ribbon down the length of the egg and tuck it under the other end. Use the remaining ribbon to make a large bow for the top. Secure in position with clear adhesive tape.

quick tips

- **This is a perfect cake for Easter, as long as you're confident about shaping the sponge into an egg shape. Once the cake is decorated it will keep well in a cool place for several days.**

- **There are quite a lot of trimmings from this cake, so keep them for a trifle or mix them with melted chocolate to make truffle cakes.**

a midsummer night's dream

serves 16

decoration time 1 hour

23 cm (9 inch) square bought or
Basic Sponge Cake (see page 9)

single quantity Buttercream
(see page 15)

8 tablespoons raspberry or
strawberry jam

28–30 cm (11–12 inch) square plate

icing sugar or cornflour, for dusting

1 kg (2 lb) lilac ready-to-roll icing

250 g (8 oz) dark green
ready-to-roll icing

20 cm (8 inch) square cake board

1 small set battery-operated
decorative lights

small bunch of wired silk foliage

small bunch of pink, purple or
cream-coloured wired silk flowers

small bunch of lavender

about 750 g (1½ lb) ornamental
cream-coloured pebbles

1 Slice any dome off the top of the cake. Cut the cake in half horizontally and sandwich the layers with half the buttercream and all the jam. Put the cake on the plate and spread with the remaining buttercream.

2 Dust your work surface with icing sugar or cornflour and roll out the lilac icing to a 35 cm (14 inch) square. Lay the icing over the cake and smooth it down the sides, trimming off the excess around the base.

3 Roll out the green icing to a 23 cm (9 inch) square. Lightly brush the cake board with water and lift the icing over the board. Smooth the icing over the sides and trim off the excess around the base. Reserve the trimmings. Position the board on top of the cake.

4 Put the battery-operated lights on the centre of the board and position the flowers and foliage over and around the lights, making sure that the lights are evenly spaced among the flowers and that you're able to activate the switch. If necessary, use the icing trimmings to prop up the flowers on the board. Scatter the pebbles over the board to fill the gaps and conceal the batteries and wires.

quick tip

- The larger the party, the bigger you can make this cake. Whatever cake size you use, the board should be 2.5 cm (1 inch) smaller to support the decoration.

fruity celebration cake

serves 28

decoration time 45 minutes
plus chilling

15 cm (6 inch) and 20 cm (8 inch)
round bought or homemade Rich
Chocolate Cakes (see page 10)

25 cm (10 inch) round plate

double quantity White Chocolate
Ganache (see page 17)

375 g (12 oz) white chocolate

500 g (1 lb) soft fruits
(e.g., strawberries, raspberries,
blueberries and redcurrants)

100 g (3½ oz) redcurrant jelly

1 Put the larger cake on the plate. Use a palette knife to spread two-thirds of the ganache over the top and sides. Position the smaller cake on top and cover it with the remaining ganache.

2 Break the chocolate into small pieces and put them in a bowl over a pan of gently simmering water. Leave until the chocolate has melted. Use a piece of string to measure the circumferences of both cakes. Cut 2 strips of greaseproof paper, each 2.5 cm (1 inch) longer than the circumference of the cakes and 2 cm (¾ inch) deeper.

3 Spread the melted chocolate over each strip of paper to within 1 cm (½ inch) of the ends and almost to the edges. Leave for 1–2 minutes until the chocolate has cooled slightly (but not started to set), then wrap the short strip around the small cake and the longer strip around the larger cake, paper side out.

4 Chill the cakes for about 30–60 minutes or until the chocolate is brittle, then carefully peel away the paper. Pile the fruits over the top of each cake, letting the redcurrant sprigs spill slightly over the sides.

5 To glaze the fruits, melt the redcurrant jelly with 1 tablespoon water until it is smooth. Use a pastry brush to coat the fruits evenly with the mixture.

quick tips

- For an even more intense chocolaty experience, make up an extra quantity of chocolate ganache and use it to sandwich the cakes together in 3 layers.

- An extra pair of hands will make the job of wrapping the collar of chocolate around the larger cake easier.

carnival time

serves 16

decoration time 1 hour

2 x 15 cm (6 inch) round bought or
homemade Basic Sponge Cakes
(see page 9)

double quantity Buttercream
(see page 15)

28–30 cm (11–12 inch) round,
brightly coloured plate

icing sugar or cornflour, for dusting

300 g (10 oz) yellow
ready-to-roll icing

300 g (10 oz) red ready-to-roll icing

200 g (7 oz) orange
ready-to-roll icing

2 cm (¾ inch) round cutter

selection of brightly coloured
streamers or ribbons and party
poppers or tooters

1 Slice the domed surface off each cake and cut the cakes in half horizontally. Use half the buttercream to sandwich the layers together. Put one cake on top of the other, sandwiching them with a little more buttercream. Use a sharp knife to cut a 'waist' out of the stacked cakes so that the stack is wider at the top and base. Put the cake on the plate and cover it with the remaining buttercream.

2 Measure the circumference at the base of the cake with a piece of string. Dust your work surface with icing sugar or cornflour and roll out 250 g (8 oz) of the yellow icing to a strip the length of the string and half the overall depth of the cake. Wrap the icing around the cake, easing it to fit where the cake is narrower in the centre. Roll out 250 g (8 oz) of the red icing and use it to cover the top half of the cake.

3 Thinly roll out the orange icing and cut it into strips, each 3 cm (1¼ inches) wide. Make diagonal cuts across the strips to create large diamond shapes. Use a dampened paintbrush to secure them around the centre of the cake and add halved diamond shapes around the base of the cake.

4 Roll out the remaining yellow icing and cut out plenty of small yellow circles with the cutter. Secure these to the cake, then arrange more circles on the plate. Re-roll the red icing trimmings to a circle, 15 cm (6 inches) across, and use it to cover the top of the cake. Pile plenty of streamers or ribbons and party poppers or tooters on top of the cake.

quick tips

- If you can't get orange icing you can make it by kneading red and yellow ready-to-roll icing together.

- Buy large bags of party poppers and streamers from party and catering stores.

pumpkin patch

serves 24

decoration time 45 minutes

20 cm (8 inch) round bought or homemade Basic Sponge Cake (see page 9)

6 tablespoons apricot jam

double quantity Buttercream (see page 15)

30–35 cm (12–14 inch) round wooden board

250 g (8 oz) orange ready-to-roll icing

icing sugar or cornflour, for dusting

15 g (½ oz) chocolate brown ready-to-roll icing

8 sprigs artificial foliage, each containing 3–5 leaves

1 Cut the cake in half horizontally and sandwich the layers together with the jam and a little of the buttercream. Put the cake on the board and spread the remaining buttercream in an even layer over the top and sides, swirling it decoratively with a palette knife.

2 Roll the orange icing between the palms of your hands into balls of varying sizes, dusting your hands with icing sugar or cornflour if the icing starts to stick. Flatten each ball lightly into a pumpkin shape and make deep grooves evenly all around the sides of the pumpkins with the back of a knife.

3 Roll the brown icing into a rope and cut it into short lengths. Dampen one end of each length with a paintbrush and secure them to the pumpkins for the stalks.

4 Arrange some of the foliage on top of the cake, nestling all but one of the pumpkins among the leaves. Arrange more leaves and the remaining pumpkin around the base of the cake.

quick tip

• The little pumpkins on this cake are surprisingly easy to make and look stunning nestling in their green leaves. They'll look even more effective if they're all different sizes, so don't be too precise.

spider's web

serves 16

decoration time 30 minutes

20 cm (8 inch) round bought or
homemade Basic Sponge Cake
(see page 9)

double quantity Buttercream
(see page 15)

33–35 cm (13–14 inch) round plate,
preferably red or orange

icing sugar or cornflour, for dusting

1 kg (2 lb) white ready-to-roll icing

1 tube black writing icing

black food colouring

15 g (½ oz) black ready-to-roll icing

1 flat liquorice bootlace

several sweet snakes or insects

orange or black candles

1 Cut the cake in half horizontally and sandwich the layers together with half the buttercream. Put the cake on the plate and spread over the remaining buttercream.

2 Dust your work surface with icing sugar or cornflour and roll out about 875 g (1¾ lb) of the white icing to a circle, 33 cm (13 inches) across. Lay the icing over the cake and smooth it around the sides, trimming off the excess icing around the base.

3 Use the black writing icing to pipe 6 lines over the top of the cake, crossing them in the centre. Working from the centre outwards, pipe curved lines of icing to resemble a spider's web.

4 Roll 50 g (2 oz) of the reserved white icing into a ball, then mould it into a ghost shape. Press the shape on to the surface to make sure it stands upright, then secure it to one side of the web with a dampened paintbrush. Paint the ghost's eyes and mouth with the black food colouring using a fine brush.

5 Make the spider. Roll the black icing into a ball and position it on the web. Cut 8 pieces of liquorice, each 4 cm (1½ inches) long, and secure 4 on either side of the black icing ball. Arrange a few sweet snakes or insects on the web.

6 Roll the remaining white icing into a long, thin rope and arrange it in a curvy line around the sides of the cake. Push the candles into the icing for support.

quick tip

• Using a tube of icing to create the web is much easier than it looks, but there will be enough icing in the tube to pipe a web on a plate if you want to practise first.

haunted house

serves 15

decoration time 30 minutes

150 g (5 oz) luxury dark or milk cooking chocolate

30 cm (12 inch) bought chocolate Swiss roll

15 cm (6 inch) bought chocolate Swiss roll

23 cm (9 inch) round cake board

3 ice cream cones

200 g (7 oz) milk chocolate buttons

125 g (4 oz) white ready-to-roll icing

brown paste food colouring

icing sugar or cornflour, for dusting

2 teaspoons smooth apricot jam

1 tube black writing icing

Halloween candles and candle-holders

1 Break the chocolate into pieces and put them into a large, heatproof bowl set over a saucepan of simmering water. Leave until just melted. Meanwhile, cut one-third off the large Swiss roll.

2 Spread a thin layer of melted chocolate over the cake board and stand all the Swiss roll pieces up on their ends so that they touch each other and resemble a castle, with the shortest piece of Swiss roll at the front.

3 Spread melted chocolate over the ice cream cones and stick them to the top of the Swiss rolls with a little more chocolate. Press chocolate buttons in overlapping rows over the cones to resemble roof tiles, beginning at the widest part of the cone and working upwards, adding extra chocolate to the back of the buttons as you near the tip of the cones.

4 Reserve half the white icing and colour the remainder light brown. Dust your work surface with icing sugar or cornflour and roll out the icing. Cut out windows, windowsills and a double door. Stick them on to the cake with a little apricot jam and use a small knife to mark the door with lines. Add two tiny balls of icing for doorknobs.

5 Knead and roll out the white icing. Cut out ghost shapes and stick them to the windows with a little jam. Add tiny white balls for eyes and pipe black eyes and mouths with writing icing. Arrange the candles and candle-holders on the cake board.

quick tips

- If you find that some of the chocolate buttons slide off the chocolate-covered ice cream cones, position just 2–3 rows on each cone to start with, then gradually add extra layers as the chocolate begins to set, sticking them on with more melted chocolate.

- If you are planning to transport the cake to a party, secure the cakes with long wooden skewers inserted through the centres of the ice cream cones, so the tops of the turrets don't topple over in transit, adding sticks at step 2.

fireworks night

serves 12

preparation time 10 minutes

cooking time about 50 minutes

decoration time 1 hour, plus drying

icing sugar or cornflour, for dusting

100 g (3½ oz) yellow
ready-to-roll icing

5 cm (2 inch) and 3 cm (1¼ inch)
star cutters

200 g (7 oz) orange
ready-to-roll icing

100 g (3½ oz) red ready-to-roll icing

20 lengths heavy gauge florist's wire,
cut to various lengths

4-egg quantity Basic Sponge Cake
mixture (see page 9)

double quantity Buttercream
(see page 15)

20 cm (8 inch) square plate

500 g (1 lb) dark blue
ready-to-roll icing

1 Dust your work surface with icing sugar or cornflour and roll out three-quarters of the yellow icing. Cut out stars in both sizes. Roll out a third of the orange icing and cut out more stars. Lightly dampen some of the large yellow stars with water and secure some of the small orange stars to them. Bend the tip of a length of florist's wire over to create a hook and push it into the centre of a star. Repeat with the other stars. Cut out more shapes, such as 'wheels' of red and yellow icing and long, ribbony shapes, and thread these on to more wires. Transfer all the shapes to a large baking sheet lined with nonstick baking paper and leave them to harden for several hours, preferably overnight. Reserve the icing trimmings.

2 Turn the cake mixture into a greased and lined tin, 25 cm (10 inches) square, and level the surface. Bake in a preheated oven, 160°C (325°F), Gas Mark 3, for about 50 minutes until just firm and a skewer, inserted into the centre, comes out clean. Leave to cool.

3 Slice the dome off the top of the cake and cut it into 4 equal pieces. Sandwich the cakes into a stack with half the buttercream and transfer to the plate. Spread the remaining buttercream over the top and sides.

4 Roll out more orange icing and cut out a 12 cm (5 inch) square. Put this on top of the cake. Roll out the blue icing and cut out 4 squares to cover the sides. Position these around the cake, pressing them together at the corners to seal. Use strips of the remaining orange icing to decorate the top and bottom edges.

5 Use the red and yellow icing trimmings to cut out ribbon and star shapes. Secure these around the box. Press the wired shapes into the top of the cake to finish.

quick tip

- Florist's wire can be easily bent to form small hooks with small pliers. It's sold in pre-cut packs or in rolls.

glacé fruit cake

serves 24

decoration time 30 minutes

20 cm (8 inch) round bought or homemade Rich Fruit Cake (see page 11)

100 g (3½ oz) smooth apricot jam

3 tablespoons brandy

icing sugar or cornflour, for dusting

500 g (1 lb) yellow or white almond paste

25 cm (10 inch) round serving plate

250 g (8 oz) selection of crystallized fruits (e.g., cherries, papaya, mango, melon, pineapple)

4–5 dates, halved and pitted

1–1.5 metres (3–5 feet) orange ribbon, 5 cm (2 inches) wide

1 Put the cake on a baking sheet. Blend the jam with the brandy and spread a little over the sides of the cake.

2 Measure the circumference of the cake with a piece of string. Dust your work surface with icing sugar or cornflour and roll out three-quarters of the almond paste to a strip the length of the string and 1 cm (½ inch) deeper than the cake. Secure the strip around the cake.

3 Halve the remaining almond paste and roll out each piece to a long, thin rope, slightly shorter than the string. Twist the 2 ropes together and arrange the twist around the top edge of the cake. Put the cake under a moderate grill for 2–3 minutes, watching the paste closely until it is evenly toasted. (Rotate the baking sheet slightly to get an even colour.)

4 Transfer the cake to a serving plate. Cut all the fruits into equal pieces. Brush the top of the cake with a little more glaze and scatter over the fruits. Brush the fruits with the remaining glaze and secure the ribbon around the sides.

quick tip

• This cake is a perfect choice for marzipan lovers or those who find icing just too sweet. You can buy mixed bags of glacé fruits, including pineapple, papaya and mango, to which you can add some glacé cherries. Boxes of whole glacé fruits are also available – although they are rather expensive – from delicatessens and department stores. These can be cut into large pieces so that the shape of the fruit is still recognizable.

christmas star

serves 12

decoration time about 1 hour, plus drying

icing sugar or cornflour, for dusting

1.25 kg (2½ lb) white ready-to-roll icing

5 cm (2 inch) and 3 cm (1¼ inch) star cutters

25 cm (10 inch) round bought or homemade Basic Sponge Cake (see page 9)

double quantity Buttercream (see page 15)

4 tablespoons smooth raspberry or strawberry jam

28 cm (11 inch) round cake board

selection of silver and gold balls

silver or gold food colouring

ribbon for edge of cake board

1 Dust your work surface with icing sugar or cornflour and thinly roll out 100 g (3½ oz) of the icing. Use the larger cutter to cut out plenty of star shapes. Cut out the centre of each star with the small cutter and transfer the stars to a lined baking sheet. Leave for several hours or overnight.

2 Cut out a circle of paper, 25 cm (10 inches) across, and fold it in half. Fold the halved paper into three to make a wedge 6 sheets thick. Make a pencil mark 5 cm (2 inches) from the point and an equal distance from the sides. Draw a line from each outer corner to the pencil mark. Cut along the lines and open out the paper into a star. Rest the star over the cake and use it as a template for cutting out a star shape. Cut the cake in half horizontally and sandwich with half the buttercream and all the jam. Spread the remaining buttercream over the cake.

3 Thinly roll out a further 275 g (9 oz) of the icing and use it to cover the cake board, trimming off and reserving the excess around the base.

4 Lift the cake on to the board. Roll out half the remaining icing and cut out long strips, each the depth of the cake. Use these to cover the sides of the cake, pushing the strips well into the corners and emphasizing the star shape by pinching the icing into points. Work in manageable strips of icing.

5 Roll out the remaining icing to a circle, 25 cm (10 inches) across, and use the paper template to cut out a star. Dampen the top edges of the icing around the sides and lift the star on to the cake, pressing the icing together around the edges.

6 Press the silver and gold balls into the top and sides of the cake and over the board. If necessary, dampen the icing with a fine paintbrush to help them stick. Paint the star shapes and arrange them on the cake. Secure the ribbon around the edge of the cake board.

quick tips

- Freeze the sponge trimmings from the cake and use them in a Christmas trifle.

- If you find shaping the cake difficult, you might be able to buy, or hire, a star-shaped cake cutter, in which case you might prefer to use a rich fruit cake mixture instead of a sponge cake.

jagged jewel cake

serves 24

decoration time 20 minutes

20 cm (8 inch) round bought or homemade Rich Fruit Cake, covered with almond paste (see pages 11 and 21 for recipe and technique)

25–30 cm (10–12 inch) round glass plate, preferably red

icing sugar or cornflour, for dusting

1 kg (2 lb) white ready-to-roll icing

200 g (7 oz) red, purple, orange and green clear boiled sweets

6 red tea lights

1 metre (39 inches) red ribbon, about 4 cm (1½ inches) wide

1 Put the cake on the plate. Dust your work surface with icing sugar or cornflour and roll out the icing to a circle, 33 cm (13 inches) across. Lay it over the cake, smoothing the icing around the sides and trimming off the excess around the base.

2 Line a large baking sheet with kitchen foil. Unwrap the sweets and space them about 4 cm (1½ inches) apart on the foil, making sure the colours are evenly mixed. Put the sweets in a preheated oven, 200°C (400°F), Gas Mark 6, for 3–5 minutes until they have melted together and are bubbling but not turning brown. Watch closely for the last couple of minutes because the sweets will quickly darken and start to burn. Leave them to cool on the foil.

3 Peel away the foil from the sweets and use your fingers to break the sweets into large, jagged pieces.

4 Arrange the tea lights in a circle in the centre of the cake. Surround these with the sweet brittle, pushing the pieces gently into the icing. Tie the ribbon around the cake and light the candles just before serving.

quick tip

- The sweets can be melted up to 2 days in advance. Once they have cooled, leave them on the foil-lined baking sheet and cover tightly with lightly oiled clingfilm. This will stop them softening and turning sticky. Once they are on the cake, the sweets should stay brittle for a couple of days before they begin to soften.

citrus candle cake

serves 40

decoration time 30 minutes

25 cm (10 inch) round bought or homemade Rich Fruit Cake, covered with almond paste (see pages 11 and 21 for recipe and technique)

30 cm (12 inch) round glass plate

double quantity Royal Icing (see page 18)

5 small clementines

5 tea lights

several small sprigs of bay leaves

5 cinnamon sticks

12 gold dragées

1–1.5 metres (3–5 feet) gold-edged ribbon, about 3 cm (1¼ inches) wide

1 Put the cake on the plate. Cover it with the icing, swirling it over the top and sides with a palette knife.

2 Cut a slice off the top of each clementine and scoop out as much flesh as possible. Dry the clementine skins on kitchen paper. The flesh sometimes comes away cleanly, leaving dry skins, in which case you won't need to dry them.

3 Put a tea light inside each clementine and arrange them around the top of the cake. Tuck the sprigs of bay leaves, the cinnamon sticks and dragées between the fruits.

4 Tie the ribbon around the sides of the cake, finishing with a bow, if liked.

quick tip

- You can cover a cake with royal icing up to 2 weeks in advance, but leave the clementines and other decoration until the day before you want to serve the cake so that they don't deteriorate.

easter chicks

makes 8

decoration time 25 minutes

8 bought or homemade Fairy Cakes
(see page 13)

double quantity citrus Buttercream,
coloured yellow (see page 15)

icing sugar or cornflour, for dusting

250 g (8 oz) yellow
ready-to-roll icing

125 g (4 oz) orange
ready-to-roll icing

16 edible silver balls

1 Remove the paper cases, spear each cake with a fork and spread the tops and sides thickly with buttercream.

2 Dust your work surface with icing sugar or cornflour and knead the yellow ready-to-roll icing. Shape 8 small balls from some of the icing and stick them to the cakes for chick heads. Dot the tops with a little buttercream.

3 Roll out the remaining yellow icing and stamp out eight 5 cm (2 inch) rounds with a plain biscuit cutter, re-rolling the trimmings as necessary. Cut the rounds in half and mark the edges with a small knife to resemble feathers. Press them to the sides of the chicks.

4 Shape tiny triangles of orange icing and stick them to the chick heads with a little water for beaks. Roll the remainder into thin ropes and cut into 16 x 5 cm (2 inch) lengths. Make 2 slits in the end of each 'leg' piece for feet and then stick the chick bodies on to the legs with any remaining buttercream. Add the edible silver balls for eyes. Arrange on a plate or cake board.

quick tips

• If you can't buy ready-coloured icing, mix white ready-to-roll icing with a little red and yellow paste colourings to make orange.

• Ready-made muffins could also be used, but, as they are a little larger, you will have only enough buttercream for the chicks. If you have tiny children, you could also make mini-versions with cakes or muffins made in petit four cases.

easter nests

makes 12

decoration time 20 minutes

single quantity chocolate Buttercream (see page 15) or Chocolate Fudge Icing (see page 18)

12 bought or homemade chocolate Fairy Cakes (see page 13)

200 g (7 oz) flaked chocolate bars, cut into 2.5 cm (1 inch) lengths

36 covered chocolate mini-eggs

1 Use a small palette knife to spread the buttercream or chocolate icing over the tops of the cakes, spreading the mixture right to the edges.

2 Cut the short lengths of flaked chocolate bars lengthways into thin shards.

3 Arrange the chocolate shards around the edges of the cakes, pressing them into the icing at different angles to resemble birds' nests. Pile 3 eggs into the centre of each 'nest'.

quick tip

• Cutting chocolate flake can be extremely messy. Use chocolate vermicelli instead.

duck, bunny and chick

makes 12

decoration time 25 minutes

single quantity Buttercream
(see page 15)

yellow and blue food colourings

12 bought or homemade Fairy Cakes
(see page 13)

2 glacé cherries

1 Put two-thirds of the buttercream in a bowl, beat in a few drops of yellow food colouring and mix well. Use a small palette knife to spread it in an even layer over the tops of the cakes.

2 Colour the remaining buttercream with blue food colouring. Transfer it to a piping bag fitted with a writing nozzle or use a greaseproof paper piping bag with the tip snipped off.

3 Pipe simple duck, bunny and chick shapes on to the iced cakes. Cut the glacé cherries into thin slices, then into tiny triangles and use them to represent beaks on the ducks and chicks, and tiny eyes on the bunnies.

quick tip

• Specialist cooking stores will stock biscuit cutters in the shape of animals and birds, which you could use to cut shapes from rolled-out coloured icing. Decorate them with glacé cherries or paint on features with food colouring and a paintbrush or writing icing.

flying bats

makes 12

decoration time 30 minutes

icing sugar or cornflour, for dusting
125 g (4 oz) black ready-to-roll icing
2 tablespoons clear honey
12 bought or homemade Fairy Cakes (see page 13)
175 g (6 oz) orange ready-to-roll icing
1 tube black writing icing
selection of tiny red, orange and yellow sweets

1 Dust your work surface with icing sugar or cornflour and knead the black ready-to-roll icing. Roll it out thickly and cut out 12 bat shapes by hand or using a small bat-shaped biscuit cutter. Transfer to a baking sheet lined with nonstick baking parchment and leave to harden while you decorate the cakes.

2 Spread ½ teaspoon honey over the top of each cake. Thinly roll out the orange ready-to-roll icing and cut out circles with a plain 6 cm (2½ inch) biscuit cutter. Arrange an orange circle on top of each cake.

3 Put a bat on top of each cake. Pipe a wiggly line of black icing around the edge of the cake. Dampen the edge of the orange icing and press the sweets gently over the black icing.

quick tips

- If you're making these cakes for a Halloween party, you could decorate them with black cats or witches' hats and broomsticks.

- Decorate the table with plastic Halloween figures or foil ghosts, pumpkins, bats and other scary shapes, all of which are available from card shops or department stores.

wicked witches

makes 4

decoration time 20 minutes

4 ice cream cones

75 g (3 oz) dark or milk luxury
cooking chocolate

4 chocolate-covered or plain
digestive biscuits

single quantity green Buttercream
(see page 15)

4 bought chocolate-chip muffins

50 g (2 oz) red strawberry-flavoured
bootlaces

4 small different-coloured soft
sweets

4 different-coloured jelly sweets

1 tube black writing icing

32 x 12 cm (13 x 5 inch) green
cake board

1 Trim the curved tops off the ice cream cones with a serrated knife and discard them.

2 Break the chocolate into pieces and melt them in a bowl set over a pan of gently simmering water. Spread a little melted chocolate over each biscuit, then spread the remainder over the outside of the ice cream cones. Stick the cones on to the biscuits to make the witches' hats and leave for 5 minutes to set.

3 Spread buttercream over the muffins. Cut the bootlaces into 12–15 cm (5–6 inch) lengths and press them on to the muffins for hair. Halve the small soft sweets, attach them to the muffin faces for eyes. Stick on jelly sweet noses and pipe on black eyebrows and jagged, angry mouths.

4 Dot the remaining buttercream on top of the bootlace sweets and stick the hats in place. Arrange the witches on a cake board or plate to serve.

quick tips

- Make these witches look even more sinister by serving them on a black china plate, a cake board covered with black paper or a black marble cheese board.

- Hats, hair and facial features can be added to scoops of vanilla or strawberry ice cream instead of muffins.

eyeballs

makes 8

decoration time 25 minutes

8 bought or homemade Fairy Cakes (see page 13)

3 tablespoons smooth apricot jam

icing sugar or cornflour, for dusting

500 g (1 lb) white ready-to-roll icing

4 green glacé cherries, halved

4 yellow glacé cherries, halved

2 black liquorice twists

red paste food colouring

1 If necessary, trim the tops of the cakes to level them. Brush the tops and sides of cakes with jam.

2 Dust your work surface with icing sugar or cornflour, knead the icing and cut it into 7 pieces. Thinly roll out a piece until it is a little larger than a cake. Drape it over a cake, smooth the top and sides and pinch each side to form an eye shape. Trim off the excess and reserve.

3 Repeat until all the cakes are covered, re-kneading the icing trimmings to cover the final cake. Press a halved cherry into the top of each cake for the iris and add a thin slice of liquorice for the pupil.

4 Put a little red colouring on to a saucer, add a drop of water and mix together. Use a fine paintbrush to paint blood vessels on the top of each eyeball. Arrange the cakes on a cake board or plate to serve.

quick tips

- This idea can be adapted by shaping a little white icing around halved green seedless grapes instead of the glacé cherries. Add a little liquorice for the pupil.

- If you are making your own cakes, add your child's favourite flavouring.

pumpkin lanterns

makes 6

decoration time 30 minutes

12 bought or homemade Fairy Cakes
(see page 13)

½ quantity vanilla Buttercream
(see page 15)

625 g (1¼ lb) white
ready-to-roll icing

yellow and red paste food colourings

icing sugar or cornflour, for dusting

1 teaspoon smooth apricot jam

1 If necessary, trim the tops of the cakes to level them. Sandwich the cake tops together with buttercream, then spread the remaining buttercream thinly over the sides and bases of the cakes.

2 Colour 50 g (2 oz) of the ready-to-roll icing yellow and wrap it in clingfilm. Colour the remainder orange using a little yellow and red paste food colouring. Dust your work surface with icing sugar or cornflour and knead the icing well.

3 Cut the orange icing into 5 pieces. Thinly roll out a piece, then put a cake pair on it so that the joins of the cake are vertical. Pleat the edges of the icing up and over the cakes and trim off any excess. Smooth the icing edges with sugar if necessary. Continue covering the cakes in the same way, re-rolling the trimmings to cover the final cake.

4 Thinly roll out the yellow icing and cut triangular eye shapes and jagged mouths. Stick them to the cakes with a little apricot jam. Mix the yellow trimmings with any orange trimmings and shape them into a thick rope. Mark the sides with a knife, then slice and stick the rope to the tops of the lanterns for pumpkin stalks. Arrange on a cake board or plate to serve.

quick tips

- If your cake board is a little battered or scratched, cover it with coloured foil or with thinly rolled out dark green ready-to-roll icing. Trim the icing flush with the edge of the cake board, then shape the trimmings into thin ropes and twist them between the pumpkin lanterns, adding leaves if you like.

- Small individual cakes can be transformed into ghostly cakes by sandwiching two together and draping them with large circles of rolled-out white ready-to-roll icing so that it falls in soft folds. Pipe on black eyes and jagged mouths.

christmas reindeer

serves 12

decoration time 25 minutes

30 x 23 x 5 cm (12 x 9 x 2 inch)
homemade Rich Chocolate Cake
(see page 10)

40 x 30 cm (16 x 12 inch)
rectangular cake board

double quantity chocolate
Buttercream (see page 15)

icing sugar or cornflour, for dusting

125 g (4 oz) light brown
ready-to-roll icing

40 g (1½ oz) red ready-to-roll icing

15 g (½ oz) white ready-to-roll icing

chocolate sticks

sifted icing sugar, to serve

1 Put the cake on a chopping board and cut it in half to make 2 rectangles, each 23 x 15 cm (9 x 6 inches). Cut one of these halves in half again to make 2 rectangles, each 15 x 11 cm (6 x 4½ inches). Finally, cut one of the smaller pieces into 3 strips, each 11 x 5 cm (4½ x 2 inches).

2 Arrange the largest piece of cake on the cake board for the reindeer body, cutting off the corners to make a curved shape. Use the next largest piece for the head and cut off the corners to make a curved shape. Overlap the head and body and tuck the cake trimmings under the top of the head to support it.

3 Use two of the smaller pieces to make the legs, cutting the tops at a slight angle so that legs are not completely upright. Use the remaining piece of cake to lengthen the reindeer's head.

4 Stick the cut edges of the cake together with buttercream, where necessary, then use the rest to cover the top and sides of the cake. Wipe any excess icing off the board with kitchen paper.

5 Dust your work surface with icing sugar or cornflour and knead the light brown ready-to-roll icing. Roll out a little and use it to cover the ends of the legs to make hooves. Trim off the excess. Roll out the remaining light brown icing and cut oval ears, about 7 cm (3 inches) long, and a smiling mouth. Put them on the cake, pinching the ends of the ears together.

6 Shape the red icing into a ball and put it on the head for the nose. Shape the white icing into 2 ovals, and press them on to the head for eyes, sticking on small pieces of chocolate stick for eyeballs. Add whole and halved pieces of chocolate sticks for antlers. Shield the cake with a piece of paper and dust the cake board with sifted icing sugar just before serving.

quick tips

- If you don't want to open a large pack of white ready-to-roll icing just to the make the eyes, use 2 white chocolate buttons instead.

- Because the amounts of ready-to-roll icing required are so small, you might prefer to divide and colour a pack of white icing.

father christmas faces

makes 12

decoration time 20 minutes

**12 bought or homemade Fairy Cakes
(see page 13)**

**single quantity plain Buttercream
(see page 15)**

**100 g (3½ oz) luxury white
chocolate, coarsely grated**

24 dried cranberries

**24 sugar-coated chocolate chips or
small-covered chocolate drops**

icing sugar or cornflour, for dusting

125 g (4 oz) red ready-to-roll icing

1 tube red writing icing

1 If necessary, trim the tops off the cakes to level them, then spread them with buttercream. Holding each cake over a plate, sprinkle with the grated white chocolate. Put it on a serving plate or cake board.

2 Press cranberry cheeks and chocolate-drop eyes on to the cakes.

3 Dust your work surface with icing sugar or cornflour and knead the ready-to-roll icing. Roll it out thinly and cut triangles, about 5 cm (2 inches) long, and press them on to the tops of the cakes, sticking them with a little more buttercream and curling the tops slightly.

4 Pipe on red mouths with writing icing.

quick tip

- **To turn an everyday tea into a special occasion, keep a handy supply of homemade fairy cakes in the freezer and decorate them while they are still frozen.**

snowy fairy cakes

makes 12

decoration time 20 minutes,
plus drying

icing sugar or cornflour, for dusting

50 g (2 oz) white ready-to-roll icing

3 cm (1¼ inch) star cutter

200 g (7 oz) icing sugar

2 tablespoons lemon juice

**12 bought or homemade Fairy Cakes
(see page 13)**

50 g (2 oz) desiccated coconut

1 Dust your work surface with icing sugar or cornflour and roll out the icing. Cut out 12 stars. Transfer them to a baking sheet lined with nonstick baking paper or greaseproof paper and leave them to harden for at least 1 hour.

2 Beat the icing sugar in a bowl with 1 tablespoon lemon juice. Gradually add the remaining juice until the icing just holds its shape but is not too thick to spread. You might not need all the lemon juice.

3 Use a small palette knife to spread the icing over the cakes. Sprinkle plenty of desiccated coconut over each cake and gently press a star shape into the top.

quick tips

- These little cakes make a lovely gift, particularly if you put them in a shallow, square box, tied with a stunning ribbon.

- These cakes couldn't be easier to decorate and are best made up to a day in advance so they're perfectly fresh when you present them to your guests.

christmas garland

makes 1 garland of 24 cakes

decoration time 15 minutes

6 tablespoons apricot jam

1 tablespoon water

24 bought fruit and nut or cranberry fairy cakes

icing sugar, for dusting

bunch of red grapes, washed

bunch of green grapes, washed

3–4 clementines, halved

3–4 figs, halved

plenty of bay leaf sprigs

1 Press the jam through a sieve into a small saucepan and add the water. Heat gently until softened then spread in a thin layer over the tops of the cakes.

2 Arrange 15–16 of the cakes in a staggered circle on a round flat plate or tray, at least 35 cm (14 inches) in diameter. Use a fine sieve or tea strainer to dust the cakes on the plate with plenty of icing sugar.

3 Fold a piece of paper into 4 thicknesses then cut out a holly leaf shape, about 6 cm (2½ inches) long. Press a holly leaf paper template gently on the centre of 4 more cakes and dust lavishly with icing sugar. Carefully lift off the templates by sliding a knife under the paper to remove them without disturbing the icing sugar. Repeat on the remaining cakes. Arrange the cakes in a circle on top of the first layer.

4 Cut the grapes into small clusters. Tuck all the fruits into the gaps around the cakes and into the centre of the plate. Finish by arranging small sprigs of bay leaves around the fruits.

quick tip

• For extra decorative effect, use gold, silver, patterned or white paper cake cases.

Index

acknowledgements

Executive Editor: Sarah Ford

Project Editor: Kate Tuckett

Executive Art Editor: Joanna MacGregor

Designer: Ginny Zeal

Production Controller: Nigel Reed

picture acknowledgements

Alamy/Adrian Franklin 11.

Octopus Publishing Group Limited/David Jordan 4 left, 7 left, 7 right, 16 right, 20 right, 24 top left, 24 top right, 24 bottom right, 24 bottom left, 27, 29, 31, 33, 35, 37, 39, 41, 43, 45, 47, 49, 51, 53, 63, 65, 67, 71, 75, 77, 166 top right, 166 bottom right, 189, 201, 209, 211, 213, 215, 217; /Lis Parsons 1, 2-3, 8 left, 8 right, 14, 15 top, 16 left, 17 top, 17 bottom, 18 top, 18 bottom, 19, 20 left, 21 top right, 21 bottom left, 22 left, 22 right, 23 left, 23 right, 55, 57, 59, 82 top left, 82 top right, 82 bottom left, 85, 87, 89, 91, 93, 95, 97, 99, 101, 103, 105, 107, 109, 111, 113, 130 top left, 130 top right, 130 bottom left, 133, 135, 136, 139, 141, 143, 145, 147, 149, 151, 153, 155, 157, 159, 161, 163, 166 top left, 169, 171, 173, 175, 177, 179, 181, 183, 185, 187, 191, 193, 195, 197, 199, 219; /William Reavell 10; /Gareth Sambidge 4 right, 5, 6, 13, 15 bottom, 61, 69, 73, 79, 81, 82 bottom right, 115, 117, 119, 121, 123, 125, 127, 129, 130 bottom right, 165, 166 bottom left, 203, 205, 207, 221; /Simon Smith 12.